HONK
IF YOU'RE AWAKE!

*poems for
a republic
in peril*

Stephen Wing

WIND EAGLE
PRESS

HONK IF YOU'RE AWAKE!
Poems for a Republic in Peril

Copyright © 2026 by Stephen Wing.
Contains no A.I. ingredients.
All rights reserved.

Book design, cover design
and collage art throughout by Stephen Wing.
All graphic images are "found art" randomly
collected by the author over many years
(see p.176).

Any opinions expressed herein are those of
the author and do not represent any
organization he is involved in.

Author photo, p.175: Gloria Tatum

Printed and bound in the United States of America.

ISBN-10: 0-9793907-6-1
ISBN-13: 978-0-9793907-6-0

Wind Eagle Press
P.O. Box 5379, Atlanta GA 31107

for my father

Doug Wingeier

a lifelong teacher

who never stopped

learning

Acknowledgements

With gratitude to:

Scenezine (Chicago) for publishing "Men Arrive to Shovel Ashes out of the Apartment Next Door" (Summer 1989)

The Open Door ministry (Atlanta) for publishing "The Hotel for the Homeless" in *Hospitality* (April 1991)

Up & Out of Poverty Now! (Atlanta) for publishing "Back of the Bus" (Nov. 1992) and "Creatures Like Us" in *Street Heat* (Oct./Nov. 1993)

The From Trident to Life Campaign for publishing "Pheasants Waking Under Glass" in its newsletter (Oct. 1994)

The Georgia Poetry Society for publishing "The Keyhole's Soliloquy" in its anthology *The Reach of Song* (Byron Herbert Reece Poetry Contest, 3rd place, 1995)

Mid-South Review (Memphis) for publishing "New Skin" (1996)

The Poetry Society of New Hampshire for publishing "Somewhere Children Do Not Play at War" in their anthology *The Other Side of Sorrow* (2006) and to *Sojourners* magazine for reprinting it (2017)

Nuclear Watch South for publishing "The President's Shadow," "Blast Radius" and "Ceremony at the Gates" in its newsletter, *Nuclear Watch Tower*

Also by Stephen Wing

Four-Wheeler & Two-Legged: Poems (Southeastern Front, 1992)

Crossing the Expressway: Poems from the Open Road (Dolphins & Orchids, 2001)

Proof of the Miraculous:
Campfire Poetry from the Rainbow Gatherings
(Wind Eagle Press, 2018; now in e-book format)

Wild Atlanta:
Greenspaces & Nature Preserves of 'The City in the Forest'
with photographs by Luz Wright
(Wind Eagle Press, 2023)

Washed in the Hurricane: Poems for an Endangered Paradise
(Wind Eagle Press, 2024)

The "Earth Poetry" chapbook series (Wind Eagle Press)

"Despotism, to reach the soul, clumsily struck at the body, and the soul, escaping such blows. rose gloriously above it. Such is not the course adopted by tyranny in democratic republics. There the body is left free, and the soul is enslaved."

Alexis de Toqueville, *Democracy in America* (1835)

"A great civilization is not conquered from without until it has destroyed itself from within. The essential causes for the decline of the republic lay in her class struggle resulting from policies favoring the accumulation of wealth by a privileged minority and the attendant alienation of the working class; the abuse and depletion of her natural resources; her failing economy and trade, due largely to the deleterious effects of the above policies of economic exploitation; the mismanagement and exhaustion of her treasury; an ever increasing dependence on resources appropriated from her empire; the relentless and debilitating warfare required to control this empire; and an ever growing bureaucratic despotism, which was initially rationalized as a need for increased protection against external threats but which ultimately sought to stifle all opposition. . . . The latter led finally to the usurpation of power by inferior, self-serving men who suppressed the principles of representative government upon which the republic had been founded and under which it had prospered."

Edward Gibbon's *The Decline & Fall of the Roman Empire* (1788)
as summarized by historian Will Durant

"If one is to rule, and to continue ruling, one must be able to dislocate the sense of reality . . . If human equality is to be forever averted . . . then the prevailing condition must be controlled insanity."

George Orwell, *1984* (1949)

"When plunder becomes a way of life for a group of men living in society, they create for themselves, in the course of time, a legal system that authorizes it and a moral code that justifies it."

Frederick Bastiat, *The Law* (1850)

> "I hope we shall crush in its birth the aristocracy of our monied corporations which dare already to challenge our government to a trial by strength, and bid defiance to the laws of our country."
>
> Thomas Jefferson, letter to George Logan (1816)

"A self-regulating market turns human beings and the natural environment into commodities, a situation that ensures the destruction of both society and the natural environment. The free market's assumption that nature and human beings are objects whose worth is determined by the market allows each to be exploited for profit until exhaustion or collapse. A society that no longer recognizes that nature and human life have a sacred dimension, an intrinsic value beyond monetary value, commits collective suicide. Such societies cannibalize themselves until they die. This is what we are undergoing."

Chris Hedges, *Adbusters* magazine (2010)

> "Tell them that we are deeply concerned about them because a country that exports repression will one day unleash that repression against its own people. A nation that wages war against the poor in Nicaragua will ignore the needs of its own poor. A country which in the name of 'democracy' fights wars against the self-determination of other peoples cannot remain a democracy. I have felt for a long time that the U.S. people will one day be the most repressed people in the world."
>
> Father Miguel D'Escoto Brockmann, Nicaraguan priest & diplomat, when asked for a message to take back to the U.S.

> > "Those who deny freedom to others deserve it not for themselves, and, under a just God, cannot long retain it."
> >
> > Abraham Lincoln, letter to H.L. Pierce (1859)

"The guilt of those who deluded one generation after another, poisoning their minds and souls with lies, is immeasurable.... Today, we are reaping the bitter fruits of our own moral laxity. We are paying for succumbing to conformity and thus to giving silent approval of everything that now brings the blush of shame to our faces and about which we do not know how to answer our children honestly."

The Soviet newspaper *Izvestia*, announcing that history exams had been canceled for over 53 million students (1988)

> "It will be said that there is no time. Yes, probably. But let me cite a remark of Toqueville. In his last work, *L'Ancien Regime*, he notes 'with terror,' as he says, how throughout the eighteenth century writer after writer and expert after expert pointed out that this and that detail of the Old Regime was unviable and could not possibly survive; added up, they proved that the entire Old Regime was doomed and must soon collapse; and yet there was not a single man who foretold that there would be a mighty revolution."
>
> Paul Goodman, "Getting Into Power" (1962)

>> "If I seem to take part in politics, it is only because politics encircles us today like the coil of a snake from which one cannot get out, no matter how much one tries. I wish therefore to wrestle with the snake."
>>
>> Mohandas Gandhi, writing in *Young India* (1920)

"I imagine that future generations will look back on these closing years of the twentieth century and call it the time of The Great Turning. It is the epochal shift from an industrial growth society, dependent on accelerating consumption of resources, to a sustainable or life-sustaining society. There is no guarantee that we will make it in time for civilization, or even complex life forms, to survive; but it is clear that there's no alternative, because now we are, in systems terms, 'on runaway,' consuming our own life support system. I consider it an enormous privilege to be alive now, in this Turning, when all the wisdom and courage we ever harvested can be put to use and matter supremely."

Joanna Macy, *Earthlight* magazine (1999)

Honk If You're Awake!

Author's Foreword	10
1. At the Democracy Museum	12
This Explains Everything	14
The Fifth Point of the Compass	15
Guided by Hallucinations	16
Blessed Are the Undocumented	18
New Skin	19
The Keyhole's Soliloquy	20
The Hotel for the Homeless	21
In the Restaurant of Earthworms	24
Welcome to the Free Market Casino!	25
Creatures Like Us	26
Never Argue with a True Believer	28
Parolee	29
The Pledge of Amnesia	30
Sparkplug	33
One Bullet, One Vote	34
Proposed Amendments to the Moral Code	36
Offertory Hymn	37
The Fortune-Teller Shuffles Her Cards	38
At the Democracy Museum	40
Babylon Sunrise	44
Blue Lights	45
In the Autumn of the Last Empire	46
The Cancer Rides for Free	48
2. The Undersecretary's Nightmare	50
"Soviet Ship Moving Toward Nicaragua May Carry MiG-21s"	52
Faultline	53
Men Arrive to Shovel Ashes out of the Apartment Next Door	54
At the Rally	56
The Undersecretary's Nightmare	57
Up Working the Night Before the War	60
The Tale She Told	64
Wedding Portrait	66
Call to Prayer	67
In the Event of My Detention or Disappearance	68
Inhabited Flesh, Haunted Bones	70

Benediction for the Dead	76
Somewhere Children Do Not Play at War	77
The Amputees' Parade	78
History	80
3. In the Presence of the Disappeared	82
4. Pheasants Waking Under Glass	110
Dead Men's Plans	112
"North to Alaska"	113
Sleeping Under the Satellites	114
The Earthquake Under My Bed	115
The President's Shadow	116
Premonition	117
Waiting for the Archeologists	118
Ceremony at the Gates	120
Blast Radius	124
Pheasants Waking Under Glass	125
The Weight of a Memory	126
Interrogation	128
5. Questioning the Interrogators	130
The World Travelers at Home	132
Happy Birthday, Buddha!	133
News for You	134
Hitler Came for the Gypsies First	135
Panoramic	136
Back of the Bus	138
Vigil in the Citadel	139
Troy Davis Park	140
Election Day on the Vernal Equinox	142
My Language and My Skin	143
Obstruction of Injustice	146
Even If We Fall	147
Questioning the Interrogators	148
In the Cracks of Babylon	156
Pause	157
What Democracy Looks Like	158
The Echo of Loneliness	160
The Whole Thing at a Glance	160
Mosquito	161
The Palaces of the Poor	162
Afterword: "Duties of the Witness"	164
About the Author	175

Author's Foreword

I live in a democracy, where time and time again, ordinary citizens have taken to the streets in vast numbers to demand change, pushing democracy slowly but steadily forward, making it more fair, more just, more democratic.

But I also live in a nation openly ruled by a wealthy elite, the infamous "One Percent," who over the past half-century have spent millions to roll back the gains of the great people's movements of the 20th century and exponentially increase their own wealth, power, and control.

During the same period, my government has expanded its military supremacy around the world through covert wars, right-wing coups, proxy dictators, bombers, troops and drones— benefiting no one except the giant multinational corporations which are no more than a façade for the same wealthy One Percent.

And since the turn of the 21st century, Republican and Democratic administrations alike have abandoned all pretense of nuclear "deterrence" to aggressively surround both Russia and China with land and sea-based first-strike forces. Vladimir Putin's brutal invasion of Ukraine, backed by the shadowy threat of nuclear Armageddon, is the predictable result.

This book is divided into sections concerned with each of these assaults on democracy, human rights, and our hopes for a just and peaceful world— right up to the current attempt to replace the Constitution with an imperial presidency, exposing at last the true intent behind decades of deceptive rhetoric. To counter the cumulative weight of arrogance and atrocity, a final section offers hymns to resistance, glimpses of heroism, and testimonies to hope.

As always, it is the poor at home and abroad who bear the brunt of my government's crimes against humanity, and ordinary taxpayers like me who pay for them. As a citizen, I recognize my responsibility to join others in resisting these crimes committed in my name, whenever and however I can. And as a poet of conscience, I find them insistently surfacing in my writing as well.

Collectively, these poems illuminate the choice we face— and have always faced— now that we can no longer evade the necessity to choose. Is the United States of America a democracy, or is it an empire? Do we meekly turn around and go back to "Whites Only," blacklists and loyalty oaths, back-yard fallout shelters and back-alley abortions? Or do we press on across this latest bridge toward Dr. King's Beloved Community?

Stephen Wing

(1)

At the Democracy Museum

"For America, if eligible at all to downfall and ruin, is eligible within herself, and not without; for I see clearly that the combined foreign world could not beat her down . . . Flaunt it as we choose, athwart and over the roads of our progress loom huge uncertainty and dreadful, threatening gloom . . . Our lands, embracing so much (embracing indeed the whole, rejecting none) hold in their breast that flame also, capable of consuming themselves, consuming us all."

Walt Whitman, *Democratic Vistas* (1871)

> "We want to fill our culture again with the Christian spirit. We want to burn out all the recent immoral developments in literature, in the theater, and in the press— in short, we want to burn out the poison of immorality which has entered into our whole life and culture as a result of liberal excess."
>
> Adolf Hitler, radio address (1933)

"When Americans think of dictators they always think of some foreign model. . . . But when our dictator turns up, you can depend on it that he will be one of the boys, and he will stand for everything traditionally American."

Dorothy Thompson, *New York Herald Tribune* (1937)

> "We are called upon to help the discouraged beggars in life's marketplace. But one day we must come to see that an edifice which produces beggars needs restructuring."
>
> Martin Luther King, Jr., "Where Do We Go from Here?" (1967)

"The American system is the most ingenious system of control in world history . . . One percent of the nation owns a third of the wealth. The rest of the wealth is distributed in such a way as to turn those in the 99 percent against one another: small property owners against the propertyless, black against white, native-born against foreign-born, intellectuals and professionals against the uneducated and unskilled. These groups have resented one another and warred against each other with such vehemence and violence as to obscure their common position as sharers of leftovers in a very wealthy country."

Howard Zinn, *A People's History of the United States* (1980)

> "If the personal freedoms guaranteed by the Constitution inhibit the government's ability to govern the people, we should look to limit those guarantees."
>
> President Bill Clinton (1993)

This Explains Everything

Deleting old voicemails
late last night,
I heard the halting voice
of my old doctor,
the familiar ring of arrogance
gone, whispering
that he was terribly sorry
but he'd made a mistake.
After lifting my aching old heart
out of its cavity
between the sawn ribs, raw
and dripping, he had hastily
sewn me up without remembering
to replace it.
                    This
explains everything.
Seventeen dead in the latest
deadly rampage
of an antisocial kid
with a semiautomatic weapon.
An ex-Marine who survived
vicious hand-to-hand combat, lost
years later to an overdose
of lethal memories.
A young girl abducted
from a shantytown in Peru,
sold into slavery in some place far
more civilized.

A whole family huddled in the wind
at the top of a freeway ramp
behind a sign that says, "Evicted.
Please help."
At last I know why none of it
makes me howl all night
at the icy vapor trails of private jets.
Or pack up and ship all
of my possessions
to an orphanage in Peru.
Or even leak one
single
solitary tear.

The Fifth Point of the Compass

The view from every window
of this square-cornered house
is a bombed-out ruin,
a barbed-wire penitentiary,
a homeless encampment,
the glitter and flare of a refinery…
So we lowered the blinds
and hung the house with mirrors,
surrendering at last
to an irresistible itch
to look at nothing but ourselves.

We've been seeing things backward
ever since.

> "And if we're not careful some lies will come true."
>
> Tariq Ansaar Aquil,
> "Writing on the Wall"

Guided by Hallucinations

The voice of the television
in the next room
jives, brags, croons, hustles, preaches
like a creature possessed
by a swarm of demons, all gleefully
fighting for control.
I lie in the dark bedroom listening
like a madman
guided by hallucinations, each
more sure of itself than I am
here in the echoing stillness of another
night alone.

                  And why not?
They inhabit a world
that generates its own light
and laughter, music and magic,
ruled by beautiful immortals
who smile affectionately into a void
thronged with shadows
all gazing in unison
through that plexiglass frontier
into the bright interiors
and sunlit scenery
of someone else's heaven,
like starving children at a banquet
of billionaires.

And who asked
for my opinion, anyway?
The celebrity pitchman's spiel,
the evangelist's patter,
game-show prattle and talk-show palaver,
the news team's banter
and the politician's deeply heartfelt
propaganda fill the quiet
like the comforting buzz
of machinery we depend on but don't
have to understand,
a conversation livelier than ours
ever used to be...

But where
could all those wrangling voices
be leading us, I wonder?
And why do we flock to that
irresistible glow
like insects around a lamp,
plunging headlong
into the luminous barrier
that divides our world from theirs,
littering the carpets
of our dens and living rooms with ghostly
silver wings?

Blessed Are the Undocumented

Night and day the chemical plumes
and industrial effluents
slip unnoticed across the borders
that people are forbidden to cross.

All night the travelers track the Pole Star
across the desert. All day
they hide from the homicidal sun.
High above them a river
of migrating butterflies points the way.

Ahead of them a broad shallow barricade
of brown water bars their path.
So many have awakened
from the dream of freedom
in that border's nightmare grip.
So many have died of dehydration, thirsting
for the shimmer of a mirage.

On the other side of the border,
malignant tumors and arterial plaque
stalk the vigilante evangelists in their easy chairs.
Politicians preach the gospel
of the lynch mob from a pulpit
constructed entirely of indigenous bones.

The fieldworkers toil all day
between the irrigation ditches
while the weedkiller drifts across in clouds
and washes steadily out of the fields
into the rivers. The bosses
lie awake at night dreaming of the day
when the field hands will labor for nothing
on both sides of the border.

New Skin

I can't feel
the blackness of his hand
inside my new leather gloves
though I remember not
noticing
if he had other gloves
when he held them out
and said he
needed money for the train

I only hesitated
the downbeat of a breath,
half a glance, and asked
if he had change for a ten
— then caught
the whisper of his friend as I
pushed through the station's
swinging door,
"You sold the gloves?"

I can't feel
the palm that sweated through
their woolen linings, the fist
that wore seams in the scuffed
black fingers,
I can't smell his color on my hand—
but I can still feel the tingle
of a living grip
that gave dead leather
life

The Keyhole's Soliloquy

Home is where your key
fits

>AMERICA DEMANDS A SUPERIOR CAULK
>*(a billboard over morning traffic)*

Homeless is yesterday's bus transfer,
brand-new jacket in the dumpster
slashed in two, a city
between concrete and wind, the view
from under a bridge

>TO HELL WITH ENGLISH ONLY,
>WE SPEAK THE LANGUAGE
>OF NOTHING TO LOSE
>>*(red letters at your window
>>on the commuter train)*

Home is when you reach your steps
and reach without thinking
to the hip pocket, the zipper in your purse
that guards your luck-charm, safety
if not salvation

>FREE VCR
>FREE LOVESEAT
>FREE CHINA
>Giveaway Days
>>*(the advertising circular
>>waiting on your doorknob)*

Homeless is the lock you turn
behind you

>PLEASE, MY LITTLE GIRL NEEDS BLOOD!
>>*(a middleclass white man begging
>>across the boulevard all day
>>and at night, floodlights)*

> "In the cage there is food.
> Not much, but there is food.
> Outside are only great stretches of freedom."
>
> Nicanor Parra, "Inflation"

The Hotel for the Homeless

The hotel for the homeless next door
is closing down,
the many-roomed mansion of brick and air
that stood for twenty years abandoned
by all but the
abandoned themselves is closing down
into a heap
of wet bricks and memories,
the long red flank of brick and broken windows
across our landlord's new fence
is collapsing into itself at last
once and for all

In the mud front yard
a hydraulic ostrich on caterpillar tracks
dozes for the night,
the new gravemound of brick and dust
well saturated now with the rain, raw mud
on tangled pipes
stacked against the fence,
rotting planks sticking out of the rubble
like the crooked gravemarkers of a civilization
gone mean and crazy at the end...

The hotel for the homeless on the corner
is closing down
after years of hanging open
like a wound,
leaning inward on itself like an old drunk
ignorant of the law of gravity,
falling piecemeal and at random into a space
consecrated somehow by the imminence
of its collapse,
a sanctuary for refugees
from loftier dangers than death—
a hole in its roof the size
of sky and sun
letting through the counsels of rain and stars,
a slab of plywood leaning in the doorway
letting through the supplicants
of loneliness and hunger

They used to sit
on its front stoop in the twilight,
smoking and talking in invisible voices,
carrying their life savings
in a paper sack
that passed from hand to hand till it was gone,
wearing their
hand-me-downs from the dumpster,
slipping in and out
through the sagging plywood
for their nightly lack of privacy…

The hotel for the homeless next door
is closing down,
by week's end the machines have left the corner lot
less than vacant, a hole in the ground
strewn with raked straw,
a doctored photograph, a history
revised, a monument
to the conscience of our time
entombed in air and an unfamiliar view
of townhouse balconies,
a brick abutment along the property line
all that's left
of the monument to ruin

Gradually I grow accustomed
to the view,
to sun all afternoon and the troubled
respiration of traffic,
to making my turn without a landmark—
but on my way
to the mailbox I remember glancing
from the shattered sidewalk,
the faces
of the shadow-dwellers, the palpable
pause in conversation and the noncommittal glow
of cigarettes,
and as I open the gate in the fence built
just for them
I ask myself where
my neighbors have gone
to bed tonight?

In the Restaurant of Earthworms

Who says the humans have no
natural predator?
The tan, lean gods and goddesses
of our cannibal age
are fattening us for some hedonistic
breakfast, never fear!

There he is,
trying to sell me sudden death
from the movie poster in the station,
slow death
from the cigarette placard on the train—
There she is,
taking aim with her swizzlestick
and cocked hips, selling me sexy death
from a billboard going by—

There they are
laughing together, dining by candlelight
in their private world
behind the TV screen, selling us
well-to-do death
through the pawnshop window
as we gather at the altar of our pawned
possessions for worship . . .

Who says we never were
the favorite of the gods?
In the restaurant of earthworms,
the scrawniest of us are guests of honor!
To feed the microscopic predators
of the soil,
ten thousand children must die each day!
And the tender ones
at the tip of the food chain, who have lived
all their lives off the labor of others—
one day it will simply be
their turn.

Welcome to the Free Market Casino!

Wait a minute.
Hand the nation over to those gamblers
down on Wall Street? Isn't that
sort of like letting the criminals make the laws?

Remember, it's the nature of gamblers, especially
the ones who are winning,
to go right on gambling until they lose.

And for every winner in the game,
ninety-nine losers
must go home and tell their wives they've lost it all.

But what the losers don't know
is that every game in the house is rigged.
The winners are the same rich, pale, ruthless hustlers
night after night.

When even they inevitably lose at last,
the dealer simply bails them out
with your grandmother's pension and deals another hand.

The cards are marked.
The dice are loaded. The books are cooked.
The criminals *do* make the laws.

Until finally one man sits alone
at the table, peering out from behind the fortified
battlement of his stacked chips.

He's looking the wrong way.
What are the odds a thief will break in
to steal his winnings
before the bloodclot in his artery reaches his brain?

Creatures Like Us

They're breathing out there
somewhere too,
the ones who make a living from the murder of Creation—
unlocking the car door, the defense kingpin—
stepping over a curb, the trafficker in waste—
you know, the ones who know
the true cost of what they're selling and still keep on
making a killing—

Can such a child be born of animal?
Do they bear a little birthmark somewhere shaped
like one more bloodstain on the map?

So they carry the musk of
extinguished species
under their fingernails— the trader
in uranium futures, the petrochemical dealer—
so the wiring in their offices is haunted
by the gravesongs of generations they sold into slavery—
Maybe they never lost someone they loved.

Are they aliens? Cold psychotics? Mutants
for a cruel millennium? Is it simply power that corrupts,
or do demons possess us after all?

No, maybe they're the last
true believers:
the millionaire with elephant blood on his hands—
the tobacco baron, lobbying the deaths-per-thousand
of loyal customers— the hamburger tycoon,
calculating how many cattle could be beef
before the topsoil is gone—

Do they carry a number from another life,
the faint tattoo of a shackle on the heel?
Are they only fresh incarnations of our pain?

Or maybe they just never loved
anyone at all:
the master of ordnance, entertaining
at the same restaurant another foreign minister
shopping for anti-personnel,
the glass in his condominium dark with eyes
of children who never saw their
mothers again—

Are they creatures like us, a feast
for microbes? Were they children once?
Do they still notice the sky?

He's out there somewhere
right now, gazing
from a private jet on the lights of his domain,
dark countryside of his mortality,
looking down on the hotel bellboy, winos
wheedling change, pigeons waddling between the steps
of indentured souls in grey suits,
maybe you, maybe me,
and maybe he wonders—

Do they recognize me up here, a scared hurrying
creature like themselves?

Never Argue With a True Believer

Never argue with a true believer!
Anything can be hammered into a weapon:
the gentleness of Jesus,
the compassion of the Buddha...
Every empire was founded on slavery.
An eye for an eye, a tooth for a tooth
fills the history books
like the holy scriptures of some doomsday cult.

An eye for an eye for an eye,
and pretty soon
no one notices the heaps of charred bones
littering the fine print of contracts,
the glint of razor-wire
around the sales floor at the big-box store—

Never do business with a true believer.
A lie can't possibly be a lie
if you believe it with all your heart.
The re-education camps are open for business
under new management!
They only want to lock you up until you learn
to love them
as they love themselves.

A tooth for a tooth for a tooth,
and before long no one blinks
when hungry jackals roam the halls
of the courthouse
and the rotating lights of an ambulance
rake the sandbox
at the children's playground—

Never fall in love with a true believer.
Anything can be forged
into manacles and chains:
the noble longing for freedom,
the open heart of democracy...
Every revolution births another tyranny.
Turn your back on the graven image
of Andrew Jackson
on every twenty-dollar bill!
Drive the money-changers from the temple
of your unblemished body!
Let him who is without sin
launch the first missile!

Parolee

The man was just
out of prison, he said, he was
soaking wet just like
newborn but he had
no one to catch him, just
wandering in the rain
enjoying his freedom to wander
in the rain as it slowly turned
to sleet, without a roof or even
a hatbrim to catch it—
Freedom is nice,
he might have added
if he wasn't shivering so hard,
*but ain't no parole
from the rain.*

The Pledge of Amnesia*

> (*title borrowed from a five-year-old boy
> overheard in the grocery store)

Beware the leader
who leads with his mouth
while an electronic eye prowls the crowd
and an invisible hand
sacks the treasury
and the bailed-out billionaires
who never paid taxes in their lives
break another rack of balls
on a table of cushioned felt
in their private club a hundred stories up
above the stock exchange...
Beware the leader who leads
with his mouth.

Citizens!
Let us plunder the land
and call it "progress"

Let's foul the water
and call it "enterprise"

Let's devastate the climate
and call it "productivity"

So sad, all this
unrequited love for money
drowned in alcohol, overdosed
on opioids... But hey,
these ticks and maggots and fleas
and investment bankers,
they're only trying to make a living,

like the rest of us!
And if people who work two jobs still can't
afford to live— isn't that
what credit is for?
So sad, all this unrequited
love for money...

Patriots!
Let us send in troops
wherever people yearn for freedom,
and call it "defense"

Let's launch a drone-strike
wherever people starve for dignity,
and call it "security"

Let's auction the government
to the highest bidder and call it
"freedom"

Everybody knows
it isn't cool to care.
So here we go again, surfing the tsunami
of the wage-price index
while wildfires rage
across the housing projects
of the condemned,
and hurricanes whip factory towns
abandoned by their factories,
and earthquakes triggered
by fracking wells
break up farms and families
eroded by drought
and debt... But never mind.
Everybody knows it isn't
cool to care.

Fellow Americans!
Let us trade our future
for stock options and capital gains
and call it "prosperity"

Let's invent a history
that matches our corporate P.R.
and call it "heritage"

Let's dig up the earth
to build a tower to heaven
and call it "America"

It's too late, that's all money
under the bridge.
Remember when
a healthy population used to be
a national asset?
We were so innocent then!
To a multinational
pharmaceutical conglomerate,
sick people are so much
money in the bank!
Remember, We
the People are the proud
engines of economic growth,
not just the lawful prey
of drooling monsters
that crouch on heaps of gold
and human bones
in carpeted fluorescent caves
overlooking the capital ...
But never mind. It's too late.
That's all just
money under the bridge.

Attention shoppers!
Let us now stand together
facing the nearest digital device
and solemnly recite
the Pledge of Amnesia:

So sad, all this unrequited
love for money

Everybody knows
it isn't cool to care

That's all money
under the bridge

Sparkplug

I do this work for you, my love.
It's my good luck that I enjoy
the doing. But it's for you.
They could have hired some other
shoeless traveler, sailor marooned
on the landlocked island of love,
knight-errant unhorsed by a lady, sworn
to the holy quest for a paycheck—
But without that pulse of fire in the veins
of lovers, not one of these towers
of commerce and industry could stand.
This contained explosion in the heart.
Sparkplug of every empire.

One Bullet, One Vote

> "Political power comes out of the barrel of a gun."
> Chairman Mao

If you think you have to bring your gun
to the polling station to win,
you've already lost.

Through the tinted windshield of the truck
with the oversized tires and the oversized flag,
it's hard to see the fear in his eyes.
Only the glint of his weapon gives it away.

He's surrounded and outnumbered
in this rabble of cheats and connivers.
But each person in line only gets one vote.
Cradling the semiautomatic assault rifle makes him feel
he has as many votes
as his magazine will hold.

So why is he so scared?
His enemies are unarmed. Uneasily he recalls
the triumphs of the nonviolent,
the bloodied faces of the marchers at the bridge,
the unsheathed mercies of love.

For thousands of years our only measure of courage
was an appetite for killing.
The sign of righteousness was firepower.
What is civilization but the advance of technology?
And what dark-skinned rabble was ever
a match for ours?

God gave us the victory! Or was it victory itself
we worshipped every Sunday?

Eventually the God of victory gave us a whole continent
soaked in the blood of people with dark skin.
So who gave all these dark-skinned people
the right to line up here
and vote? It can't be fair
to win back a continent with courage alone!

His finger curls around the trigger
like a caress. This time will be different.
This time the bullets will spell out precisely what he can't find
in all the words he knows.
This time love won't make it across that bridge.

But bridges are built to overcome
old habits of separation.
The banks of the river have long since forgotten their differences.
He feels his grandmother watching, the one
who's still alive. His other grandmother watches too.
Their love surrounds him like a soft blue halo.

Each person in the line wears the same halo:
children, wives or husbands, elders
living or dead. But if he squints down
the sights of his gun, they're only dark silhouettes
on a target range.

"Love your enemies," his Sunday School teacher
used to say. *But this is Tuesday*,
whispers his fear.
He tightens his grip on his gun.
He holds his enemies too close to let them go
that easily.

If I was that scared, I guess I'd carry one too.

Proposed Amendments to the Moral Code

Shall the morally handicapped be granted
a permit to park
in the holy sanctified
handicapped parking space
beside the front door
of all licensed establishments of trade?
Don't bother.
They'll park there anyway.

Shall self-worship be granted protection
under the Freedom of Worship clause
of the First Amendment
in the Bill of Rights?
Doesn't matter.
The self-ordained and self-canonized
have long since privatized
the entire Constitution
and all its concomitant codes and decrees.

Shall the Church of Mammon be granted
official tax-exempt status
under the duly executed Tax Code
of the United States?
Never mind.
The Internal Revenue Service has been
a dutiful subsidiary
of Mammon, Incorporated, for decades now.

Shall the aforementioned incorporated entity
be granted the sacred privileges
of legal personhood
and multinational citizenship?

Too late.
It has already revoked
the personhood and citizenship
of the rest of us,
and is now busy drafting
a retroactive repeal
of the Emancipation Proclamation
and the Declaration of Independence.

This time around of course
the legal ownership of slaves
shall not discriminate
by race, gender, religion, sexual orientation
or ethnic origin.
We've come too far for that.
When you hear your number called
over the loudspeaker,
step up on the docket and strip, turn in place
under the spotlights
and smile.

Offertory Hymn

This world is my church.
All of it.
And these beggars
along the freeway ramp are only
passing
the offering plate.

> "The time of manifest destiny is over,
> the time of grief has come."
>
> Robert Bly, "Anger Against Children"

The Fortune-Teller Shuffles Her Cards

The livestock train shudders through
my sleeping neighborhood at midnight

"All aboard!" the rumble and clatter
of steel against steel seems to call across
the dim jurisdictions of streetlights and stars
to the thousand dreaming households
crowded along the tracks

*and the sleepwalkers rise from their beds
to obey the injunction of the court,
weeping, bewildered, guilty as charged,
lining up for the tattoo and the lash
and unknown horrors beyond . . .*

But as any fortune-teller can tell you,
the sun never goes away
without a promise— the tiny child
who climbs a child-sized tree, the leaf
that turns even toward the dying
of the light—

"Wake up!" sing the brakes in that aching
falsetto you can feel in your teeth,
then fall silent again as the wheels
of the nightmare rattle on and recede
into the next neighborhood and on
down the line

*and my slumbering neighbors stumble
back to bed, shivering and yawning*

*— all but the innocent illegals, who shrink
into the shadows of the platform to wait
for their own passage to the slaughterhouses
of the animal holocaust, where they work
their daily shifts of blood and terror
to supply the sacrificial lunch-meat
of the ignorant elect . . .*

And I lie listening to the dwindling echo
of cattlecars through some future midnight
I'm just beginning to remember, and pray
I'm not the only one awake and listening
and remembering

as the digits tick away toward dawn,
toward the re-awakening of not just light
but awareness, the opening
of not just eyes but understanding,
the resurrection of not just memory
but vigilance—

*And the fortune-teller shuffles her cards
under the candleflame and tries again*

At the Democracy Museum

Come in!
Why stand out there
in the hurricane?
Hang up your hazmat suit,
your Kevlar vest,
peel off the sterile mask and gloves,
make yourself comfortable!
Let me show you around.
Here in the lobby, our collection
of broken glass
and used hypodermic needles.
Note the blood-spattered
linoleum, designed
by Kissinger himself.
Look, this skinful of splintered bones
was an elected foreign leader!
Down the hall a glass case
of campaign stickers and pins,
Fourth of July fireworks and parades,
a whole room
full of worn-out promises
and old attack ads ...
Careful, don't leave fingerprints
on the glass!
We collect those too.

This was once a democracy
on every channel. Now
every other November we get
re-runs.

Come in, come in!
The food court is open to all
major credit cards,
regardless of race, religion, gender,
or sexual perversion.
We were just sitting down
to a game of drones
and a bottle of Agent Orange,
pull up a chair!
Ignore the waitress chained to your table
by her pitiful wage. The gag
across her mouth,
the protest signs in her eyes—
all part of our reconstructed period decor.
A warm plate of waterfowl
with petroleum sauce
is waiting in the microwave.
Just drop your tip in the hat
when the homeless veteran comes limping
from table to table
on his prosthetic limbs.
In the gift shop next door,
an assortment of souvenir scalps:
Apache, Vietcong, Muslim
and Mexican, both domestic
and fieldworker . . .

Democracy is a place found only
on old maps
of the future, where secrecy
is a foreign language
and obedience is treason.

Please, come right on in!
The elevator only goes down
at the moment,
but it's the only free ride
in the building.
Here in the basement, our gallery
of interactive exhibits.
Blow the dust off that antique
voting machine,
drop in a quarter and pull the lever,
watch the twin columns
of grinning faces spin past.
You can't lose, we've stocked it
with Hollywood's most smooth-spoken,
sun-tanned and blow-dried,
branded, sponsored,
scripted and teleprompted
impersonators of leading men.
Don't forget to salute
whenever the vintage color TV
in the corner pans across Old Glory,
our state-of-the-art
security cameras don't
miss a thing!

Those who would trade what's left
of their freedom
for a little temporary
convenience, whispers the face
on every hundred-dollar bill,
deserve neither.

Where
do you think you're going?
I said, come in!
On your left,
our world-famous wax-figure tableau
of the billionaire industrialists
with their leashed packs
of lobbyists.
Behind you, shadows of the lynch mob
by torchlight, permanently
mounted on the wall.
And finally, here
in our open-roofed atrium,
a life-size display
of Minuteman missiles, still aimed
at their traditional targets,
authentic rusty drums of strontium-90
leaking in the background.
Feel free to join in as we sing
reverently
in praise of the heroes
of old black-and-white war movies
and denial of the holocaust
to come.

*So what would you rather say
to your children, if
and when the day finally comes
when nothing you say matters,
even to you? "See, I told you so!"
or "Forgive me, I did
what I could ..."*

Babylon Sunrise

Driving home in the dawn,
the city skyline still burning its lights
as all the colors
come stealing into the world
for the very first time again,
indigo, violet, lavender,
I ache...

For every smiling corpse
surrounded by flowers
in a funeral parlor,
another lies twisted on the ground
still grimacing with the taste
of agony, unmourned
as yet—

Let us pray
it's no one we know.

Silhouettes of tree-limbs
reach over the freeway,
black as the memory of midnight
across the ripening day,
magenta, vermilion, apricot,
the delusion of eternal darkness
dying its slow daily death
across my windshield
one more time...

Some of us end our days
in posh clubs for the elderly,
surrounded by loved ones
and the machinery of life-support.
Some of us end up in the back room
of the police station, hanging
from a pair of handcuffs, quietly
hemorrhaging—

*Lord help us
stay out of trouble!*

The sky glows all around me
like an enormous rose in full bloom,
delicately tinting the world
the color of violated flesh
just before the blood
as I make my way home
over shining streets
through the daybreak...

Amen.

Blue Lights

The armed guardians
of public morality smell your fear,
sniff the liquor on your breath
as you roll past and on
down the highway in the dark,
probe your smoking ashtray
with psychic radar,
pull out behind you and ease
into traffic like some lady
at the bar with blue lights
flashing in her eyes

In the Autumn of the Last Empire

I have heard there are people
who lived their whole lives
and died
without a single car wreck or bankruptcy
or divorce, who never wasted away
with terminal cancer,
never ran for cover
from a high-altitude bombing
of their particular suburb
or lost a limb
stepping on a land mine

I pledge allegiance to the U.S. dollar bill
and to the massive private wealth for which it stands:
one nation deep in debt, divided against itself,
with unlimited credit
and mandatory entertainment
for all

In one corner of the flag
a blue lifeboat
sails away to heaven, bearing
the saved souls of white folks
escaping just in time
from a continent scraped down to nothing
but the sun-bleached parallel stripes
of highways, the canals
filled with fresh blood
between...

I have heard there are places
where people do not fear the police,
where politicians do not
fear the people,

where fear has not yet replaced loyalty
as the common coin of the realm,
where the citizens still feel free to speak
out loud
without taking the precaution
of stepping outside

I pledge allegiance to the power elite of America,
and to the profound fear of democracy
that emanates from Washington like a bad smell:
one world economy, insatiable,
with radioactive electricity and obsolete
appliances for all

And what if someone else's misery
was the cost of my happiness?
What if the bravery of young Americans
was wasted
extinguishing the dreams of foreigners?
What if we used our freedom
mostly to prey on the freedom of others,
our prosperity
to extort the world's last rupee, dinar and centavo
for ourselves?

In one corner of the flag
an orderly crowd of white folks
splashes, sinking
in a square blue pool of soulless vacuum
while behind them clear, sweet rivers
shine white in the sun,
running down to the shore
through red fall woods
in the autumn of the last
empire...

The Cancer Rides for Free

The baby born during the Philippine Insurrection
>is a great-grandmother now, delicate and gentle,
gazing back through the cobwebbed windows
of ninety years—

When palaces fall the dictators pale
>and shrivel into squeaking indignant dolls,
old footage in the vault, loose pages
flapping the streets

And when the people take the palace in
>tour groups of a dozen all day, visiting
the dungeon where their missing shoes were kept,
touching holes in a wall where
prisoners disappeared,

A silent flag hangs at half-staff
>all that night in the rain: a vigil
at the grave of an unborn grandchild
kindles in their eyes

They watch over us, happy tourists
>clicking our cameras in the monsoon light,
sailors clapping and whistling in the nightclub
where the feathered dancer smiles
and remembers

The face of our dictator does not yet grin
>from every public wall, but his decrees
blink in neon above the wet street tonight
and only the wet street hisses
a reply

Somebody's great-grandmother rides the subway this morning
>*in rouge, all dressed up for the doctor,*
blows blue smoke over her embroidery of days
while nestled in her ribs the cancer
rides for free

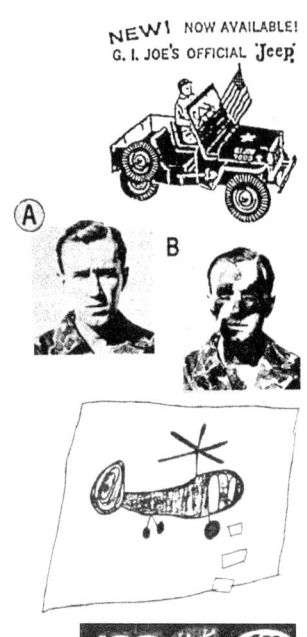

(2)

The Undersecretary's Nightmare

"When you draw near to a city to fight against it, offer terms of peace to it. And if its answer to you is peace and it opens to you, then all the people who are found in it shall do forced labor for you and shall serve you. But if it makes not peace with you, but makes war against you, then you shall besiege it; and when the Lord your God gives it into your hand you shall put all its males to the sword, but the women and the little ones, the cattle, and everything else in the city, all its spoil, you shall take as booty for yourselves; and you shall enjoy all the spoil of your enemies, which the Lord your God has given you . . ."

Deuteronomy 20:10-14

> "We surely cannot deny to any nation that right whereon on our own government is founded— that every one may govern itself according to its own will . . ."
>
> Thomas Jefferson, letter to Gouverneur Morris (1793)

"The problem after a war is with the victor. He thinks he has just proven that war and violence pay. Who will now teach him a lesson?"

A.J. Muste (1941)

> "We have about 50% of the world's wealth but only 6.3% of its population. . . . In this situation, we cannot fail to be the object of envy and resentment. Our real task in the coming period is to devise a pattern of relationships, which will permit us to maintain this position of disparity without positive detriment to our national security. To do so we will have to dispense with all sentimentality and daydreaming . . . We should cease to talk about vague— and for the Far East— unreal objectives such as human rights, the raising of the living standards, and democratization. The day is not far off when we are going to have to deal in straight power concepts. The less we are hampered by idealistic slogans, the better."
>
> George F. Kennan, "Review of Coming Trends: U.S. Foreign Policy, 2/2/1948" (declassified in 1974)

"We have had years of this war, clogging our television tubes and our heads with horror. . . . And yet one could hardly claim that the eyes of men have wept for the victims because of what those eyes have seen. Indeed an opposite claim might be made; that one televised war has prepared our souls for all kinds of future horrors."

Daniel Berrigan, *Night Flight to Hanoi* (1968)

"Soviet Ship Moving Toward Nicaragua
May Carry MiG-21s"
> (*New York Times* 11/7/1984)

and America has just re-elected
    its president.
I am riding among commuters
    on the 5:50 out
through the suburbs in the early dark.
    Over the rows
of custom-tailored shoulders I catch headlines
    but no details
as the pages of the late editions turn.
    Outside my window,
past a sleeping brunette
    reflected in fur and mascara,
the headlights burn in patient queues
    at the crossings.

Some boys in letter jackets drinking beer
    on their way to the game
watch the train go by from one of those
    dark cars.
Two of them will die in a hot country far from home.
    Only one
will see his enemy in time to realize
    it is a mistake.

Around me their pale fathers
    get up one by one
leaving me my choice of the papers to read.
    I stare out the window.
The dark comes earlier
    each year.

Faultline

Dressed in their blue and
yellow against the green, armored
in helmets and padding
with no enemy in sight,
they're practicing: the scrimmage,
the snap, the scramble,
the adolescent rush
of adrenalin against adrenalin

The field is a ladder of white
lines they skip lightly
up and down, blacks and whites
kicking their cleats
at the blue air as if the lines
are no more than paint
on clipped grass
(but the grass has been
around longer and it
knows better)

Funny how we've built a whole
civilization on the same
long fracture, crosstown rivals
coast to coast, a youthful
collision of loyalties,
these innocent
rehearsals for war

Men Arrive to Shovel Ashes
out of the Apartment Next Door

>   Yes, tonight
>   you watch alone, so you look away
>   just
>   before he touches her
>
>   But someone has lost that one tonight
>   who burns inside suddenly so much more
>   than memory
>   though less than ashes
>   or ink

Because in that country no
sympathetic landlords come visiting the wreckage
from Uptown, making notes for the insurance lady—
Because there they have declared
independence from the old landlords of the conquest—

>   Across the tossing ocean
>   of the lonesome and sleepless this night one lies
>   remembering
>   the glance of daylight, her dark
>   touch

Because in this country the landlords live on
in jealousy and spite, in that other country the soldiers came
to burn what their masters cannot have—
Because the masters live still by conquest and can't
abide the happiness of lovers—

Someday you want your
own
so you drop your gaze when she calls across the park
to a new walker suddenly
running

But someone is caressing over and over
three names
that sound like sobbing
in a foreign language, squeezing a small, soiled
tennis shoe
against the pulse in his throat

Because the wires in our walls are old
and overloaded, and the landlord never checks his messages—
Because a silence is leaking from the gas-lines—
Because we pay no mind to what is invisible and deadly
to the happiness of children

Across the sea of the despairing
someone buys four candles that will burn to nothing
by daybreak
while in his nightmare,
the helicopters return: this time dropping
only
endless flowers without scent

— the fumes of melting plastic will overcome us tonight
or some night soon, our alarm clocks
will hiss on the burning dresser
and never wake us, our chemical empire
will smother us in our beds before the flames
ever touch us

At the Rally

How difficult it is to look
an astoundingly pretty woman in the eye
while an amplified voice repeats
the word *campesino* when that is
the single instant her eye is given you
to fill your glance with whatever
she may be searching for among the eyes—

She prefers to remain a stranger.

Your sadness is not only for the children
who bear the witnessing of murder
in their eyes, for children somewhere
perhaps in that very instant of her eyes
becoming their own mothers and fathers,
for children playing in the rags
of elder brothers and sisters who have
gone seeking refuge among strangers—

They have become strangers themselves here.

No, you also mourn a child lost
between that glance and blank response,
the instantaneous life sometimes
conceived between strangers, that moment's
complicity of eyes among the crowd
that can give sanctuary: you mourn
a woman you see disappearing
into a room in her head where someday
she will lie turning memories like this one
over and over until somebody comes
to turn the sheets—

                    It's too late.
That person too must necessarily
remain a stranger.

The Undersecretary's Nightmare

> *Children Without Parents.*
> *Mothers of the Disappeared.*
> *Utterances in no*
> *human tongue.*

Men in the uniform
of the crowd, soldiers
of the secrecy of money,
some quiet account you keep
      in the Caribbean:

Their mouths hiding
the charred kisses,
shattered smiles, songs
sliced out, a cement-block
building at the edge
      of the capital:

Their mirrored glasses covering
the gravepits of the unburied,
holes in the skull that go
down the long cool corridors
underneath your desk
      in the Pentagon:

Their pockets hide
a cut of the trade,
the cigarette for burning,
razors for the necessary
      severing—

The way they stand
hides nothing.
They are loitering here
    for you.

The first stranger that looks
is your closest friend.
Quick: signal with an eyebrow
everything you ever wanted
    to remember.

> *And the neighbors vanish*
> *into the catacomb of silence*
> *between the stitched lips of the dead*
>
> *and our glances burrow deep*
> *behind the black glass*
> *in the eyes on the side of the road*
>
> *and the broken hands*
> *take root in our stomachs every time*
> *we swallow and keep walking*
>
> *and the forests*
> *of the disappeared reach up*
> *out of the ravines as we pass*
>
> *and our hearts go tumbling down*
> *with the loose-jointed dance*
> *of the no longer useful*

Into that squat cell
the size of a skull they may
shut you, you who let them
fold the limbs of a man you did not know
into half a cage—

    You crouch
at the bottom of the dark well in his eyes
and after all the knotted years at last
begin to stretch—

    The silence of the martyrs
crowds the cell so even memories
lack space to move, curled awake
you print each name over the others till the night is
black with them—

    And the features of your face
grow brittle to the touch as pictures
in old newspapers as you begin
to understand:

    Your own
disintegrated breath will be a small
ungainly appendix to this slow digestion
of the dark

> *The Vanished Children's Fund.*
> *Mothers of the MIAs.*
> *Utterances in no*
> *human tongue.*

Up Working the Night Before the War

>My love sleeps
>uneasily without me,
>a dark doorway away

>The clock ticks
>deeper into the silence

The trucker who hauls the warheads
is finishing his coffee, feeling for change.
Outside his truck shudders and waits.
The dew is about to fall.

>She breathes on, deeper and deeper

The security guard at the weapons plant
checks his reflection in the john.
The stars are invisible beyond the floodlights.

>God Bless Our Troops
>Cinnamon Brooms $3.50

>*Faint light*
>*from the other side of the world*
>*Something's burning*

Because it is prudent
sometimes to lie,
the President is putting on his underwear.
He is dressing for his rehearsal.
The makeup man arrives to paint the ritual mask.

>*I was asleep*
>*and forgot about the bomber*
>*continuously in the air since I was born*
>*I woke up dreaming you were with me*

The President's speechwriter knows us well.
He spent years selling deodorant to stockbrokers
and insurance to prostitutes
who smelled death's bad breath under their arms.
He autographed a million pictures of movie stars.

> *Tomorrow we may be*
> *ashamed of this laughter*
> *Tomorrow we may*
> *mourn this holy power to touch*

Yes, the cameras lie. It's their business
to choose the glimpse of this day
we will all remember, fix it
in a frame of light and drown the rest
in darkness—

> *Bury*
> *the hopes of corpses in a box of darkness*
> *Burn the heaps of broken hearts*
> *in a furnace of darkness*

> > "Roaches crawled over my chicken
> > right in front of my guests!
> > Never again, thanks to Combat!"

Waking up in the pharaoh's tomb at midnight,
crawling out of the tar-pit,
crushing buildings with every step,
the United States of America goes on a killing spree.
The camera crew sprints across the runway.
Crowds wave flags on every overpass.

We doze all night, flying
high above the ocean, boys in uniforms
carrying our playing cards and prayerbooks,
our sweethearts and hangovers,
rubbers and bayonets—

A hole inside you, cut with a backhoe
in the shape of a friend who didn't come back.
Enemies peering from the eyes of the one that did.

ADVO ASKS...
HAVE YOU SEEN ME?
Age at Disappearance... Age Progression...
Over 50 children featured have been recovered

> Her voice is now a child's, now a wise
> old woman's
>
> Her hair turns dark to
> light to dark
> to light
> Her eyes go grey, green, blue
> grey, green, blue

> > *No, those people*
> > *are not waiting there*
> > *to murder me*

Put it under the
false bottom of your coffin,
ignorance of the crime is no excuse:
the cold foot of the floor
against your foot,
that tingle in the groin
when you hear tales of mutilation,
the rumormongering of war—

> *"PAID FOR BY THE U.S. ARMY..."*
> *Get off my radio!*
> *As if everyone doesn't know*
> *who pays for it*

Her body regulates its temperature

The blood goes on pulsing
through her sleep

What you don't understand, Senator,
is that our species needs
two feet to stand—
a single pedestal can only hold
a statue—
and what is necessary sometimes to hold the balance
is the unexpected
step forward

> $25,000
> Bad Credit OK
> Next Day Closing

My love sleeps
uneasily without me,
an everlasting darkness away

She dreams that I am right here
in the next room, working

The clock ticks on
deeper into the silence

January 1992

The Tale She Told

*The Marines are looking
for a few good men
who will do as they're told*

The smiling presidents of
small, friendly nations
with medals on their uniforms
and silver teeth,
each one fingering in his pocket
a human spirit
stamped upon a coin, just
waiting to be spent—

*Eat, drink and sleep
with your weapon, the next clip
always ready at your belt*

Great bombers gliding
night and day across
desert and jungle, each bomb
tucked under their wings
an unsuspecting
city block somewhere, swinging
like a pocket watch
ticking on a chain—

*Some things are simply
impossible to understand
with that death-grip on your gun*

Day after day the killing
around you
builds up in your brain
like a bubble of gas
in the intestines till it bursts out
through your trigger-finger
into the tender viscera
of miscellaneous
strangers—

*The tale she told
moved a muscle in your face
that never moved before*

Suddenly you feel her hunger
opening inside you,
a bottomless falling
just below the diaphragm, her grief
like a hole in your chest
where your heart is suddenly
visible, discreetly
pumping away

Wedding Portrait

The hired killer
drives to work in his remote-controlled flying cubicle
Stops at the service station
to squeegee flecks of human tissue
from his windshield
Fills his tank with sixteen gallons of human blood
enough to fly to Yemen or Afghanistan
and back
by quitting time

In the wedding portrait, the bridegroom
lies under a heap of bricks
The bride
sprawls across the bodies of her
teenaged sister and a cousin
The blood
drains away through secret underground channels
to the other side of the world
where it collects in a hidden tank
under the concrete apron of the service station
outside the Air Force base

The killer cashes his check
every other Friday
I hardly notice the dollar and a quarter it cost me
to murder a child
I stop at the light
at the top of the ramp to offer about that much
to the veteran with the sign that reads
I served
my country, now I can't
get to sleep without a fifth of vodka, can you help
end the nightmares?

But the nightmares fly on
every night
through my dreams and yours, those dreams
of democracy,
of churches and schools, flags and crosses,
families smiling from portraits
on the wall in the den
like the one of Mom and Dad's wedding day
Grinning there among the guests
the killer they hired
to handle security while they raised their kids
and paid their taxes every April

Call to Prayer

Glittering under the streetlights
like confetti,
bits of shattered plastic line the curbs
of the intersection
where someone died today.
High above,
the lights of a jetliner cross the dark sky.
Under a brazen noon
on the other side of the world,
neighbors dig through rubble
for a missing child.
The howl of the ambulances
sounds the call to prayer.

In the Event of My Detention or Disappearance

I'm sorry,
your badge has no authority here
or anywhere
after so many billyclubs and canisters of tear gas.
You'll have to show me a gun.

I'll always remember this sky
framed by buildings
that were never so alive, ancient stone
freshly gilt with living sun

Mother taught me
always be polite to the man with the gun,
but never forget
my great-grandfathers were free.
You'll never convince her I was born for slavery.

I never saw a pair of unbeautiful eyes,
only blindfolded glances,
one-way-mirror stares,
sunglasses like patches of shadow worn
to hide behind

The handcuffs don't pretend
they represent the will of the people.
You, on the other hand,
can only fake the metallic efficiency of steel.
In the end you speak for no one
but yourself.

*In the minutes
or decades that remain,
I'll never forget
certain faces, precious laughter,
exquisite music,
bluegreen mountains rising through clouds,
that first juicy bite into a peach—
even your hands
perfect as a folded pair of wings
holding the gun*

You can build as many
prisons as it takes
to teach your children obedience.
You'll never strangle
the urge toward happiness
that pumps their blood and mine
and yours.

*No matter what you choose
to do to me,
you can't escape the beating
of your own heart*

Inhabited Flesh, Haunted Bones

1.

The elderly woman on the telephone
has a brand-new granddaughter,
I can hear the baby-laughter
tickling her voice
and the legions of bombers lift off
one by one from the runways

The church is lit with stained-glass
snapshots of the life of Christ
as we rehearse for the wedding,
bride and groom aglow
among somber stepchildren
in everyday clothes
and the bombs begin to rain down on Iraq

On crewcut lawns and flagstone patios
across the country I love
charcoal burns in barbecues,
the odor of charred meat
calls families together for grace
around the grill
and the hospitals of Baghdad
begin to fill with cries of agony and grief
and innocent
gushes of blood

Two hundred and eighty million people
watched two buildings burn and fall
in New York City,
    then watched it again
and again and again,
as many times as it took to numb the loss
of three thousand innocents.

*They walked on in a trance
of lost innocence,*
                         blindly
*retracing the steps
of some previous century's habits and routines.*

*But the fire burned on underground
in their sleep,*
                     the leaping martyrs
*rose again on toxic clouds
night after night, while
black magicians gathered in the War Room:*

*"Only a massacre of innocents
can avenge the massacre of innocents!"
they chanted to the crowds*
                        still hypnotized
*by endless re-runs of the apocalypse—
"Blood sacrifice for blood sacrifice!
Repayment of fire
in fire,*
       *with interest!"
A high-altitude lottery of shrapnel
and concussion:
resurrection of the dead Savior
to be murdered once more*

    2.

These trillion-dollar global corporations
fly the flag I love
like rogue battleships turned pirate,
firing their death-deals
like so many missiles
each tipped with five hundred Hiroshimas,
targeting the towns and cities
that harbored them along the way:

Free Trade agreements and World Bank loans,
sweatshops and toxic dumps,
paid-off cabinet officials,
death squads, killer drones
and if all else fails,
crates of depleted uranium rounds
and armor-piercing shells...

The honor of criminals
is once more at stake
so the young men strap on weapons,
leave their warm wives at home
and take up
target practice.
A soldier's job is to obey.

A citizen's job is to question:
the bulletscarred banners,
bloodstained bunting
over the review stand at the parade,
the flag on the anchorman's lapel—
even the medic is part of the disease!
Even the schoolteacher
reciting her litany of old wars,
marching her fourth-graders single file
through the shabby halls—

The man driving the Wells Fargo truck
waiting beside me at the light,
dark behind his bulletproof glass,
must sit up late
gazing into the cool flicker of television light,
all those headlines bursting
in rapidfire salvos through his brain,
and wonder
who his enemies are...

And the young woman with the tattoo
and the navel ring
who might have become a casualty
in a layoff
at the land mine factory
if her elected leaders had signed and ratified
a certain piece of paper—
inhabited flesh, haunted bones
make us blood brother and soul sister,
kin to all the fallen martyrs
of the minefields:

I have no quarrel with you.
You're making a living.
I've looked into your eyes on a bus somewhere.
I've seen you laughing.
My quarrel is with those who make
five hundred times your living
and think it's not enough.
The architects of incineration.
The evangelists of revenge.
Fire-addicts. Blood-junkies.
The ones who would lay waste to the sun
if they could only get there—

Beware, sister.
The ones who pay your hourly wage
with stolen wealth,
are they the trustees of your pension fund?
They'll shove you bodily into the breech
of the cannon
the minute their ammunition runs low.
They'll lay waste to your soul
if they can only get there.

Be sure to donate alms for the dead
while you're here,
leave a little something
for the scavengers when you go,
and you may yet be forgiven
for casting your only vote
into a lake of fire…

   3.

"How's it going?"
Irrelevant question
when children suffer amputation
without anesthesia
in bombed-out hospitals,
while farmers starve
and entire nations strangle
on insurmountable debt.
Nevertheless, we ask it:
"How's it going?"

Peace march:
rich neighborhood to poor.
Cold to sunny.
Hardly anybody looks.

Couldn't it be that the unnamed,
undefinable pain you feel
any time you stop to feel
is simply your share
of the general background level of misery
drifting out from the prisons
and slaughterhouses and refugee camps?
On the inside of my face
I am not smiling. Nevertheless, I repeat
the ritual response:
"I'm fine, how've you been?"

Silence by the tomb
of Martin Luther King.
A flute plays "Amazing Grace."

Each of us has been given
one hand to hold the candle,
one hand to shield it and
when the wind blows it out anyway
some neighboring pilgrim
with another candle
to rekindle the flame:
"Nice to see you again..."

Echo of the drum
off concrete and glass.
Peace bubbles up in my breath,
my heartbeat a slow-drumming
reply—

4.

It may be time at last to turn
and eat the Earth.
Devour it stone by stone.
Gorge ourselves on the rich dirt.
Sautee the twigs
in a delicate mudpuddle sauce,
toss the seashells in a dressing
of treesap and quicksand.
Gulp down the last living specimens
of plant, animal, insect, algae, protozoa.
Eventually each other.
Finally, ourselves.
And in the end, even our rusty junk
might flavor a salty broth
of silence.

April-May 2003

Benediction for the Dead

The wind blows in from the north
like an uninvited guest
at a funeral.

The flag ripples proudly at half-mast
above the widow's veil
of memories.

Jets banking in formation overhead
rip the morning in two.
The wind

blows the dust and smoke away
and the buildings lie
where they fell.

Someone is shrieking out a benediction
for the dead on behalf
of the living.

Across the street, someone is struggling
to remain among the breathing.
Someone else

is desperately hanging on to agony,
terrified of what might come
after.

And someone comes home with a piece
of the war embedded like shrapnel
in his brain.

Corpses rot on the parade ground.
Medals glitter in the overgrown
grass of graves.

It's too late to organize a protest march
or a victory parade. Too late
to write a eulogy.
Too late.

Somewhere Children Do Not Play at War

You can't blame me for flinching
back against the wall
when a small boy points his
pistol at me and yells "Pow! Pow! Pow!"

I am lying back there somewhere
feeling the sidewalk as if I'd never touched
sunshine, pumping out my urgent
puddle

And when three kids dash by, invisible
in their camouflage sneakers,
chattering on their walkie talkies,
pay no attention if I button my opinion
and pocket my fingerprints

I crouch somewhere in a black, sweaty
silence too small for me,
listening to voices muffled by cinderblocks
or years

And when I wake this morning
to jubilant cries, and look out to see twins
in miniature green berets waiting
while a man in uniform
unlocks the station wagon,
forgive me if I drop the curtain and start
smuggling my unborn children across the border

Somewhere I am waiting for my daughter
to come home, holding grief in
like one who holds a breath too long
under water

The Amputees' Parade

*To those who forget that armed insurrection
is an inalienable right,
according to the Declaration of Independence,
a message from a few pacifists
out here in the woods...*

It's one right nobody can take away,
as long as officers of the peace
carry guns:
to go down in a blazing crossfire
in the parking lot,
chanting to the deputies
and the flashing lights
like early Christians from their crosses,
like the witches in their turn
from the stake—

*Forgive them, O Earth, O animals, O children
for they know not
how they hurt themselves when they harm you,
it springs from inside, so deep, so long, so steady
they thought it was part of them—
please, God, forgive them their pain and let them cease
to lash it like a tail,
going down like the last dinosaur,
let them spare these youngest ones
the stalking vampire Leukemia,
the concentration-camp Starvation, the homicidal claw
of Shrapnel—*

Let them come to their senses
and see the amputee on the curb
outside the drugstore who will work for food,
counterpart to the amputee
on a street-corner in Ho Chi Minh City, formerly Saigon,
two good legs between them,
swinging forward
on their crutches in the long march of amputees
who have carried this whole damn
empire of skyscrapers and powerlines this far
anyway—

We know you have all the guns.
We know you're borrowing money in our name
every year to pay the interest
on what you've already borrowed to buy more.
But there comes a time in the course
of human events
when the earth quakes
and the people wake up, and on that day
you'd better hope a few pacifists are out here
on a mountain
praying for you

History

Not so long ago
a fire swept across this
hilltop cemetery
high in the wilderness

Blackened trunks stand sentinel
over gravestones of the nameless
and the named,
the mourned and the forgotten

Green needles sway breezily
above them
against the passing of clouds
and human generations

One monument chiseled and carved,
decorated bravely
with the torn and solitary flag
of an army long defeated

The others only flat rocks
planted upright
in the dirt,
standing crookedly on end

Speechless, indifferent,
unmarked
except for a dapple of lichen
and the green stain of time

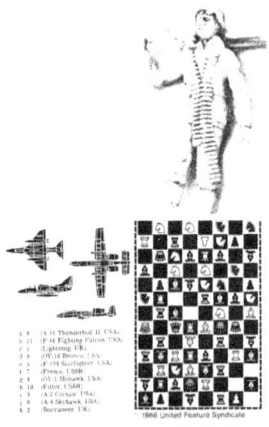

(3)

In the Presence of the Disappeared

"We have pacified some thousands of the islanders and buried them; destroyed their fields; burned their villages, and turned their widows and orphans out-of-doors; furnished heartbreak by exile to some dozens of disagreeable patriots; subjugated the remaining ten millions by Benevolent Assimilation, which is the pious new name of the musket; we have acquired property in the three hundred concubines and other slaves of our business partner, the Sultan of Sulu, and hoisted our protective flag over that swag.... And so, by these Providences of God— and the phrase is the government's, not mine— we are a World Power."

Mark Twain, *North American Review* (1902)

> "I helped make Mexico, especially Tampico, safe for American oil interests in 1914. I helped make Haiti and Cuba a decent place for the National City Bank boys to collect revenues in. I helped in the raping of half a dozen Central American republics for the benefits of Wall Street. The record of racketeering is long. I helped purify Nicaragua for the international banking house of Brown Brothers in 1909-1912. I brought light to the Dominican Republic for American sugar interests in 1916. In China I helped to see to it that Standard Oil went its way unmolested."
>
> Major General Smedley Butler, USMC, *War Is a Racket* (1935)

"It is curious that the Americans, who calculate so carefully on the possibilities of military victory, do not realize that in the process they are incurring deep psychological and political defeat. The image of America will never again be the image of revolution, freedom, and democracy, but the image of violence and militarism."

Martin Luther King, Jr., quoting an unnamed Vietnamese (1967)

> "Why were our countries insulted, invaded, and humiliated on more than 200 occasions from 1840 to 1917? Under what pretext, since at the time there was not a single socialist state in the world and the Czar ruled over all Russians?"
>
> Daniel Ortega, president of Nicaragua, addressing the United Nations (1981)

"The West won the world not by the superiority of its ideas or values or religion, but rather by its superiority in applying organized violence. Westerners often forget this fact, non-Westerners never do."

Samuel P. Huntington, *The Clash of Civilizations & the Remaking of World Order* (1993)

My Vacation in Colombia

I went to Colombia to visit my long-lost relatives. On my planet, all the inhabitants are one family, so it was easy to spot them when I arrived. Communication was another matter; I speak almost no Spanish at all.

Going to Colombia was not a plan I made. I went because the opportunity came along, and I have always believed in accepting invitations. The opportunity came because Colombia's half-century of civil war has given it the highest rates of murder and abduction in the world, fueled on one hand by petroleum and cocaine exports to the United States, and on the other by the import of billions in U.S. military aid.

As in other Latin American countries, in Colombia a wealthy minority is working with the U.S. government, multinational corporations, the World Bank and the World Trade Organization to consolidate ownership and control. Over the past 20 years, thirty million peasants have been displaced from their lands, which have been added to the holdings of the wealthiest landowners. Thousands have been massacred or "disappeared." This is why Christian Peacemaker Teams maintains a presence in Colombia, and sponsors four delegations a year like the one I joined.

If you mention to someone in the States that you're going to Colombia, you'll get a certain look, followed by a shaking of the head. In Colombia, you get exactly the same response if you say you're going to the city of Barrancabermeja, north of Bogota. So that is where we went.

C.P.T., an initiative of the Quakers, the Mennonites, and the Church of the Brethren, also has teams in Iraq, Palestine and Chiapas. I am not a Christian myself, but it was a privilege to meet real Christians, both Colombian and North American, who do honor to their founder. I hope they are not offended by my ruminations on Christianity in this poem.

Our group of twelve spent two days in Bogota, then flew to Barrancabermeja for two days, took a three-day boat trip upriver, spent two more days in Barranca, and two final days in Bogota. We met with church groups, women's groups, union groups, human rights groups, villagers in the countryside, and a U.S. Embassy official.

After the rest of the group departed, a Colombian friend accompanied me to the city of Pereira for a visit with two other friends, a pair of brothers I had met during their studies in Atlanta years before.

I found the people of Colombia warm and hospitable, even when I'd left my translators behind and couldn't understand a word they said. Their daily courage in the face of terrorism will inspire me for a long time.

October 2003

> *"Lo unico necesario el triunfo de los malvados,
> es que los hombres buenos no hagan nada."*
>
> Edmund Burke
> (on the wall at the union hall)

In the Presence of the Disappeared

1. BOGOTA

(Colombia's capital, Bogota, is 8,500 feet above sea level and has more miles of bicycle lanes than any other city in the Americas.)

From the summit of Montserrat,
the city stretches so far
up, down, and across the valley
that it disappears in mist
whichever way you look

So the tourists who ride the cable car
up for the view today won't see
the miles of suburban
shantytowns— *las casas de carton*—
that surround Bogota like
a siege of orphans,
an hour's bus ride away.

Blood of the struggle

Inside a white cathedral at the top
of the windswept stairway,
a white man with long blond hair
wearing a gilt brocade sarong
kneels where he has fallen,
encased in plate glass
above the altar, one hand
already nailed to the cross—

> *Bodies of the martyrs*

While in the back of the church,
electric candles flicker
over black steel boxes,
chained and padlocked,
with generous slots for donations,
while plaques of every size,
shape, style, material
and workmanship line the walls
pledging eternal gratitude
for miracles granted—

> *Wine and bread*

And on a sister summit nearby
the Virgin of Guadalupé,
carved in dazzling white stone,
blesses the endless *barrios*
with outstretched arms
on behalf of the steep green slopes
behind her— the Andes,
untamed by the steel strut
of high-tension electric towers.

I stand here feeling strangely
safe, looking back,
far from the left-wing guerillas,
the right-wing paramilitaries,
the extrajudicial executions,
the forced conscriptions,
the aerial fumigations,
the kidnappings and massacres,
narcotrafficantes and *terroristas*
right, left and center...

But even now I feel it:
like a shadowy shroud woven entirely
of names never called aloud
that shimmers invisibly against the sunlight,
I feel the crowded, suffocating
presence
of the disappeared.

Peace is my country, wherever I find it.
I left a nation at war
to go looking.
Not that I understood this then,
standing on the bloodsoaked
land of my birth.
I came to Colombia
because of a lifelong habit of saying
yes. And here,
among the poorest victims of war,
my country was waiting.

2. BARRANCABERMEJA

(The river port of Barrancabermeja, on the Magdalena River, is the center of Colombia's oil and gasoline industry, and an epicenter of violent conflict. Christian Peacemaker Teams maintains an ongoing presence there.)

> "Thank you for coming to Colombia,"
> said the businessman
> sitting next to me on the little
> propeller plane, after I explained
> that my business here
> was peace. His was petroleum.
> Together we watched as
> a break in the clouds revealed only
> more clouds: then a darker
> mountain ridgeline: at last
> the green *campo*, the countryside,
> disappearing and appearing,
> eventually solid enough
> to land an airplane on.

The official greeter in Barrancabermeja
is the airport crucifix,
pinned to the wall high over our heads.
Blood of the struggle
But the unofficial greeter
is the airport kitty, slipping in and out
through walls designed
like most walls in Barranca
for maximum ventilation.

Buzzards are already circling
the scent of sweaty *gringos*,
but the flock of yellow taxicabs is
quicker, and before we know it
we've joined an uptempo dance
of bicycles, motorbikes, buses and taxis
through the one-story neighborhoods
of Barrancabermeja, tripping
into some non-Euclidean space
between metaphor and hallucination.

Each bus is painted to outdo the others,
blaring popular tunes.
Every traffic median is a market,
colorful baskets of fruits and vegetables
innocently extending the curb—
the guitar vendor, seven
guitar-cases strapped to his body,
a man pushing a pig in an orange T-shirt
on a two-wheeled cart,
a bright green bird on a TV antenna,
open-air Bingo—

That first night in Barranca, while we slept,
three men and a woman
were assassinated on those streets.
Fourteen, we learned, in the past ten days.
Bodies of the martyrs
Executed without the dignity
of a trial, without even the indignity of arrest.
Eight others had simply
disappeared,
a slow, quiet, poisonous form of torture
for the ones left waiting.

> *"Don't look for the assassins.*
> *We killed him. You have one hour*
> *to resign from the union or die."*

Back home, only presidents and statesmen
are deemed worthy of "assassination."
Here it's union organizers,
teachers, soccer coaches, ministers...
But once you meet them you understand:
these who are threatened with death
for their love of the living
are easily the equal of a president back home,
as far as character goes—
sweet-faced *hombrés* with eyes
that shine like pools of coffee
or petroleum, an office full of women
whose laughter erupts like sugarcane
from riverbottom earth,
a plump *padré*, preaching
against the sin of *machismo* with emotion
dug from the coal mines
deep in his chest,
one *Colombiano* dark like chocolate,
one pale like cocaine
working together for the return
of the disappeared...

> "*Any liberated person can create liberty
> in any given space.*"

Courage has a face:
it's no abstraction here.
So many died.
Their photographs line the union hall.
Like the eternal flame
atop the highest tower of the refinery,
the impossible example
of too many fallen
compañeros y compañeras
burns on.

> *"When the moment comes for sacrifice,*
> *both leaders and members are ready."*

In the front of the church,
a long-haired white man with no nipples
hangs bleeding against
a giant street-map of three parishes.
It doesn't occur to me till after
the priest has said the early-morning mass
and passed the Eucharist—
Wine and bread
And maybe it never entered the minds
of the brown-skinned ones
around me— how their ancestors
mistook Cortez and Pizarro for gods,
and brown people have been
dying for white people ever since.
Why not grant them, at least
once a week, a glimpse of one *gringo*'s
perpetual death-agony, one at least
dying for them?

> *"A mother of a* para *hurts just as much*
> *as a mother of a guerilla."*

But even here in the church,
beneath the murmur of prayers
en Español, I can feel it:
like waves of whispers that echo
in the vast underground caverns
of unheeded conscience
under skyscrapers and factories, steadily
wearing away the bedrock, I feel
the unexplainable, undeniable presence
of the disappeared.

*Colombians killing Colombians
down in Colombia is none of our
business, it's tempting to say. But business
is exactly what it is—
sugar, cocoa, coffee, cocaine, coal, petroleum—
the addictions that built empire
after empire and called it
"civilization." And who can claim
a life or livelihood untainted
by the lies of history?
Down here in Colombia they call denial
by name: the ancient*
Lei de Silencio, *the Law of Silence.*

3. THE RIVER OPON

(Displaced when right-wing paramilitaries took over the area, several small fishing and farming villages along the River Opon have now returned home from the nearby city of Barrancabermeja, with the accompaniment of Christian Peacemaker Teams.)

>Now I know how the driftwood feels.
>Running fast and flush
>with last night's rain, the river
>carries its floating cargo of sticks and debris
>in perfect formation, smooth and serene.
>Even pushing upstream in our
>outboard canoe of welded steel,
>I feel the pull of the river's journey down
>to join the Magdalena, learn to float
>effortlessly homeward with every breath,
>so that stepping ashore
>over one of the dugout canoes
>tied along this muddy bank
>since ancient times, I still feel its current
>bearing me along.

(Blood of the struggle)

On cool, clean-swept dirt floors,
in the shade of
soot-blackened ceiling-thatch
walled with hand-cut planks
that barely show the marks of the chainsaw,
they welcome us to the *campo*
with rice, beans, beets, and fruit fresh
from the trees in the front yard:
smiling people of every
shade of brown, from riverwater to topsoil,
surrounded by just as many
persuasions of green,
one man petting a bright parakeet
that rides his shoulder
while chickens, ducks and pigeons
scramble for the tidbits we toss—

> *"Why is such a rich region so poor?*
> *Why in a region that loves life so much*
> *is there so much killing?"*

It's a beautiful river, señor.
But where's the trash?
The occasional scrap of litter
startles me, all the more strange
for the unfamiliar logo
and brand name *en Español*.
Grapefruit, orange, banana, lime, guava,
coconut, cacao, papaya, starfruit,
corn, bean, plantain
all come with packaging that efficiently rots
into rich, dark fertilizer.
The earth is so alive here,
the fenceposts take root and sprout leaves!
The corn in every field stands
twice as tall as I am!

Such a beautiful country, señor.
But where are all the tourists?

> "Colombia has had a death machine
> for political killing for many years."

(Bodies of the martyrs.)

"Paz sin Armas, Paz sin Miedo"
plead the banners tied
every so often between the trees
as we stroll with our hosts
along the riverbank—
"Peace without Arms, Peace without Fear."
Two of them we find split
precisely down the middle: not sliced,
just rotting in the tropical humidity
as fabric will. As the fabric of *la paz*
too often has. One banner
has been knotted back together;
soon the other one is.

> "The peace process
> was frustrated by both sides."

Skipping over the open water of Lake Opon,
past flocks of waterbirds in flight
and swooping electric cables,
gradually we can make out the main
village, swarming with soldiers.
Only when we land our canoes do we see
the boyish adolescent faces
peering out of crisp new jungle fatigues,
from behind heavy black steel
weapons, smiling, scowling, shy—
the same colors and expressions
as all the other faces we've seen,
but only one haircut.

> *"Women don't give birth to children for war.*
> *We're the ones*
> *who have to bring back the bodies*
> *and put them in the ground,*
> *without any way to do it.*
> *So often we don't even have time to cry."*

The *campesinos* of the world—
the peasants— seem to have no choice
but courage. They stay,
enduring everything, no matter what—
where can they go?
—until it's time to flee for their lives.
They carry what they can, bravely
abandoning all they know.
And still, again, forever, where can they go?

We *gringos* have no choice, either.
We can't escape
the invisible privilege
that automatically accrues to pale skin
almost anywhere in the world.
But some have found a way
to put even this to good use.
They call it "accompaniment":
one of the few known
treatments for the disease
of displacement,
preventive medicine for the epidemic
of assassination.
And a year after the people of the Opon
began to come home
to their cornfields and fruit trees,
their soccer fields and schools,
the army finally arrived
to guarantee their "military security."

> *"It's a lie that the government is winning the war. The only solution is political, and neither side wants it."*

Ah, this is truly and simply the lap
of luxury: porcelain!
It doesn't even have to be
white. Who needs a tank,
a ballcock, a handle?
The rain barrel is right outside the door,
its dipper dangling, the two-story
concrete cistern casting
long-legged shadows across the dew
while water swirls, vanishing
into a septic tank under the long grass,
and the sky ripens from papaya
to mango...

    (Wine and bread)

The jaguar roaring in my tent
turned out to be someone
snoring two tents over,
but still I carry home with me
my relatives the heron, the cormorant,
the egret, two macaws
flying over the river at dusk— trees
that branch in unexpected directions,
orchids blooming along their limbs,
hundreds of feet up—
the bamboo, plantain, yucca, sugarcane
that line the shore as we chug
back downstream, and
the occasional homestead
where someone invariably waves—
the horizontal tree over the water
that points out how to live
in balance
on a steadily eroding riverbank
in the Colombian *campo*—

> *"Peace is: a life of dignity,*
> *the right to food and shelter."*

But up on the empty soccer field
next to the graveyard
overlooking the lake,
like a thundering of horses so far away
I heard it only with my feet,
like a shiver traveling up my bones
to rattle my jaw against my skull
and wake my tongue,
like a tingling in my lips
and fingertips I could feel
the solemn, helpless
presence of the disappeared.

The innocent Americans
can't imagine that anyone
in a suit and tie
would ever lie to them.
But every murderer needs an alibi,
and if your government
was still spending your taxes
to exterminate whole tribes,
languages, cultures
from the endless frontier,
wouldn't you really rather be
the last to know?
La Lei de Silencio.
What you pretend not to know
doesn't hurt.

4. BARRANCABERMEJA AGAIN

(After losing a soccer match to some of the village players, our delegation returned to Barranca for two more days of meetings with non-governmental organizations, and to create a ritual on the waterfront enacting our response to what we had seen and heard.)

> The river of yellow taxis too
> seems swollen with the rain,
> its hosanna of horns
> and incense of exhaust fumes
> even louder and smokier
> after the quiet of the *campo*.

Two-wheelers are everywhere,
darting past the cars and buses,
all the motorbike riders in their helmets
and numbered vests—

Every sloping street becomes
its own gutter when it rains.
The sentinel pigeons desert their posts—
not the paramilitary spies
watching the waterfront.
The buzzards give up their circular
patrols— not the runners
for the paramilitary protection racket.
It's known as "Secure democracy."

> "8,000 *pesos per month to the* paras
> *for so-called 'security.' Where is the state?"*

A little boy sitting in front of his papa,
learning to steer the motorbike—

Yet no one will say the guerillas
were much different.
Some even switched sides
when the takeover came. Now I start to see.
The lines down the center of the street
are guidelines, not boundary lines.
Motorcycles weave down the middle
on whichever side is empty at the moment.
"Democratic security," it's called.

> *"The definition of a civil war depends*
> *on the legal status of the armed actors."*

A man with a dog trotting beside him,
tied with a plastic string
to the spare wheel mounted
on the back of his motorbike—

Green and fertile, mountainous
and tropical, cursed with veins
of buried riches, Colombia
is a natural market for guns.
Once you're armed, why work for a living?
Foreigners bleed off four-fifths
of the profits every year, anyway.
Sending money home from exile
is the second-largest industry!
On someone's map of the future,
new hydroelectric dams
export power to California, flooding
ancient Andean valleys, a new canal
links the Amazon to the Pacific . . .

That universal gesture,
rubbing all four fingertips across
the tip of the thumb—
the ideology of narcoterrorists
and multinationals alike.
"Secure democracy," they call it.

> *"Drugs are the most powerful engine*
> *of struggle in Colombia."*

A man pedaling his bicycle
carrying a stack of reclaimed lumber
across his shoulder—

Spanish is a lover's
language, says the song.
So where does a translator find the words
for death by dismemberment,
hired killers with chainsaws,
pregnant women slashed open,
body parts delivered to loved ones
in a garbage bag?
Blood of the struggle
Remember, this is what we watch
for entertainment
back home, between commercials
for all our other addictions...
It translates, "Democratic security."

> *"The judicial backlog is extreme.*
> *Impunity is the biggest problem."*

A family on their motorbike,
man in front, woman holding on, little girl
sandwiched between,
baby riding on his mama's back—

Where are the detectives
to investigate these murders?
Lined up back to back
from prime time to the late night re-runs
in a country that sends down
billions in military aid to stop the violence,
year after year after year!
Bodies of the martyrs
And what crooked bookkeeper keeps track
of expenditures for chainsaws
and garbage bags
to improve the business climate
by eliminating unions down south?
Enter it under
"Secure democracy."

> "*Privatization is coming. We can't stop it.
> We can only resist to save our dignity.*"

*A man on the back of a motorbike
towing a load, one handle
of the wheelbarrow in each hand—*

Not just for complaining after the fact,
the horn is an instrument
as essential to the drivers here
as steering wheel or brakes.
An extra yellow light always heralds the green.
But the true secret of the impromptu
choreography of these streets
slowly seeps in. No traffic cops
enforce the signs and stoplights.

The drivers seem to simply
trust: some in Jesus and the Virgin,
the saints and angels, some
in nothing but the other driver's
naked will to survive—
some, perhaps, in the eternal
closeness of death.

> "Recipients of U.S. military aid
> must be cleared of human rights violations
> by every agency in this Embassy."

*The rented washing machine, arriving
on a trailer towed by a motorbike—*

Pale virgins stand in solitary shrines
along the country roads,
some with holy babes in arms,
as if continuously
begging the blessing of Heaven
on helpless passengers,
innocent pedestrians, unarmed
children and other bystanders . . .

> "We hope you won't get tired— the situation
> will get worse. Your cards and letters
> have saved lives in this region."

*A woman waiting behind her husband
on a motorbike at the light,
loosely cradling a toddler on her thigh
who stares with wide, calm eyes
through my window
till we both begin to move—*

Wine and bread

Of course, the only slow taxi
is the one you catch
when you're late for the airport.
But even there
in the back seat,
like an invisible cloud of witnesses
testifying to the crimes against them
in a voice like a pursuing wind,
even there you can feel it:
the untraceable, inescapable presence
of the disappeared.

To murder the innocent
only betrays your fear.
But the Blackhawk helicopters
and M-16s are just the first wave.
In any war against civilians,
the key objective is the conquest
of hope itself. Padlock
the schools! Barricade the hospitals!
Restructure the economy!
Privatize! Deregulate!
Some foreign corporation is busy
trucking in fiftyfive-gallon
drums of poison as we speak—
"Hey! Need a job, señor?*"*

5. PEREIRA

(Pereira is a city in the coffee-producing region, where the violence in Colombia crops up only rarely. Friends who grew up there took me to a hot spring nearby.)

> The man next to us
> on the commuter jet
> spends the whole flight muttering prayers.
> My friend laughs. But who knows?
> Odds are, it's a rare flight that doesn't carry
> at least one person praying.
> And who can prove those aren't
> precisely the planes that go down?

Rocky escarpments west of Bogota
disappear in cloud fragments
that gradually solidify as we lift away.
The big river I can occasionally see
winding below my window dead-ends
into an even bigger one:
"The Magdalena," another passenger
informs me from the seat ahead,
practicing his English.
"Colombia's Mississippi."

Water droplets
find each other somehow, high in the air,
accumulating slowly into shapes
they never tire of improvising
till the lush, grief-stained land disappears
under a peaceful country
of sunlit cirrocumulus towering
over vales of shadow—

> *"It is the obligation of the Colombian government*
> *to provide a situation where we can*
> *determine our own destiny."*

Greasy footprints
out on the wing of the plane,
invisible a moment ago,
catch the sun all of a sudden like
hieroglyphs of fire, and once again I feel
the silent, watching
presence of the disappeared.

* * *

As every soldier must be prepared
to shoot on command,
marksmanship be damned,
a true poet must be ready
to fall in love at a glance, deeply,
gratefully, at least
once or twice a day— but here
in this country of wild *mulatto* beauty
wherever I glance I sense,
peering from the deep
subterranean shadows
of long black braids and Indian eyes,
the unseen, unmistakable presence
of the disappeared.

> *"As punishment for defying them,*
> *they cut all the hair off kids and women,*
> *even their eyebrows."*

* * *

The waterfall comes
splashing so gently down
from so far above,
pausing only
to pirouette a moment
on every pinnacle of its
descent
like some daredevil ballerina,
that it immediately
makes me want to pee.

In the open-air men's room
on the third floor of this
little brick hotel
at the end of a gravel road,
the toilet tank is running.
It doesn't seem to matter here,
cupped in this steep
forested grotto
reverberating with the endless
padded steps of falling water,
green bursts
of blooming vegetation
crowding the slopes, as if each leaf
has just this instant been born—
banana leaves, elephant ears,
bamboo, palm, palmetto, and one
solitary evergreen, stiff and formal
like a lone tourist in evening wear
among the natives—

Beside the white banisters
and potted plants of the hotel,
above the cataract
where the waterfall thunders through,
a steaming hot spring comes plunging
into one end of the pool,
a cold clean shower crashing down the rocks
at the other. And as if all that
is not enough,
the hotel hospitably provides
rock 'n' roll *en Español*
via loudspeaker, powered
by a mountain rivulet
piped into a humble red-painted shed:
the hotel's own private
hydroelectric plant.

The unarmed security guard
out at the gate only searched my bag
for liquor— forbidden competition
for the bar inside.
At the airport, leaving Barranca,
they searched it three times!
We are far from the gun-toting narcos,
the union-busting thugs,
the army units operating out of uniform,
the assassins and kidnappers
of left, right and center,
far from the mercenary cropdusters
down in Putumayo
saturating coca plants,
vegetable plots and children alike
with poison from the sky,
far from the paramilitary raids
on Indian villages across the border
in Venezuela and Panama—

But even here, lying back
in the warm pool, sipping the best
tapwater I ever tasted,
I can feel it:
like a phantom host of small
rainbow-feathered angels
singing their majestic chorus at sunrise
in total silence, I still feel
the patient, unrelenting presence
of the disappeared.

The rumble of a mountain river,
hand-made spoons and spatulas
slotted on their nails,
scrap lumber pile out back,
the smile of a stranger
as he hands you a plate— some things
are the same wherever you go.
But tell that to the Sunday Christians who are
stockholders the rest of the week,
studying their portfolios like Holy Scripture,
tracking their numbers like beads
of a rosary, faithful
all their lives to the sacred vow:
la Lei de Silencio…

On the drive back to town,
    the mountains around us
gradually disappear in the arriving
    rain.

Blood of the struggle
    Bodies of the martyrs
        Wine
            and bread

(4)

Pheasants Waking Under Glass

"It is not probable that war will ever absolutely cease until science discovers some destroying force so simple in its administration, so horrible in its effects, that all art, all gallantry, will be at an end, and battles will be massacres which the feelings of mankind will be unable to endure."

W. Winwood Reade, *The Martyrdom of Man* (1872)

> "This government holds the view that any general bombing of an extensive area wherein there resides a large population engaged in peaceful pursuits is unwarranted and contrary to the principles of law and humanity . . ."
>
> U.S protest message after Japan's bombing of Nanking (1937)

"We have had our last chance. If we do not now devise some greater and more equitable system, Armageddon will be at our door."

Gen. Douglas MacArthur (1945)

> "Ours is a world of nuclear giants and ethical infants. We know more about war than we do about peace. We know more about killing than we do about living."
>
> Gen. Omar Bradley, Armistice Day speech (1948)

"I made one great mistake in my life, when I signed a letter to President Roosevelt recommending that atom bombs be made."

Albert Einstein, letter to Ronald W. Clark (1954)

> "The taproot of violence in our society today is our intent to use nuclear weapons. Once we have agreed to that, all other evil is minor in comparison. Until we squarely face the question of our consent to use nuclear weapons, any hope of large scale improvement of public morality is doomed to failure."
>
> Richard T. McSorley, S.J. (1976)

"Formerly the future was simply given to us; now it must be achieved... The nuclear peril makes all of us, whether we happen to have children of our own or not, the parents of all future generations."

Jonathan Schell, *The Fate of the Earth* (1982)

> "I think I have reached the stage where I could die at peace and accept that reality. I could even accept the death of my children because I know they have to die sometime. What I absolutely cannot accept is the death of life on the planet. We may be the only life in the whole universe."
>
> Helen Caldicott, M.D., *Missile Envy* (1986)

Dead Men's Plans*

(*title borrowed from
a defunct detective novel)

*In an orderly universe, life
is an improbable event*

Mannequins in rabbit masks
promenade the store windows downtown
for Easter, boys in camouflage
pajamas try out new toy guns
on Christmas morning

*In a world composed
of random caroming particles
it's no accident that fifty madmen
rule an empire of blueprints
and radar screens*

A bitten thumbnail
is all that shows of the moon
to the few sane souls who glance up
cruising through silent intersections
under blinking signals at midnight

*On a planet perpetually turning
into jeweled darkness and
back to light again, it's no surprise
that half of the inhabitants
never turn to look*

Streetlights bend in the storm
like one-armed dancers,
flowers decorate a stalled escalator,
blue flames burn alone on corners

*In a sane country, life
is programmed even into the machines
In ours?*
          Dead men's plans

"North to Alaska"

John Wayne fell in love once and
                    wouldn't
admit it, even to himself (and that
was the *comedy* part—)
                          sat and
got drunk all by himself like a big
dumb sore loser—
                      meanwhile of course
someone swindled him out of his claim
(this was the drama)
                      and when he
finally figured out who it was, well
he punched the guy into the mud.

A muddy street brawl was that picture's
happy ending.
                  John Wayne kissed his
mud-spattered bride and they rode off
on a paddlewheel steamer.

John Wayne stood waving at the rail
to all America,
              drawled the secret
dream of every true American
down to the last deadpan line of "North
to Alaska." Gun. Gold. Blonde.

Now he's dead of radiation poisoning,
they've tasted oil in Alaska
and I grow afraid.
              I grow afraid.

Sleeping Under the Satellites

for Judy & Jim

Dogs yipping at the horizons of sleep
        faint
like stars going down

Moon shining through mosquito-screen
        cold
as the hoarfrost of space

How small our fabulous lives must
        look
from the satellites!

Too cold for crickets tonight, much
        too cold
to lie here in this sleeping bag

Bright enough to roam the woods
        down in
the creek bottom by dream-light

Night and day the silver geese go over
        without honking
carrying our grandchildren's cancer

Too cold and clear to sleep tonight,
        so close
to the gulf of vacuum

The Earthquake Under My Bed

I dreamed I felt the earthquake
that could split the century,
a sudden savage lurch along the fault
between mind and heart—
and woke up wondering if the light
would answer to the switch,
if I would even recognize the world
beyond the dark frame of my window
when the sun came up.

                             Transported
by a shuddering beneath my bed,
I looked down on the waking fires
of rage and pain, the black gaps
in our rational townships where history
had splintered like the beam of a roof,
spilling darkness into daylight like
the ugly jelly of a skull. Who knows
what joy or sorrow, truth
or imagination once lived in there?

But whatever contention of forces
had broken my sleep must have slipped
to a new compromise. I lay still again
beneath the rubble of my dream. I slept.

The President's Shadow

A man in a dark suit walks
six paces behind the President.
A dark briefcase handcuffed to his arm.
A black wire dangling behind his ear.

His suit is the shadow of skyscrapers
over the projects.
His briefcase is the stretched and sewn skins
of whole dark families.
He looks out through glasses
darkened by all he has orders not to see.

Inside his case he carries the long
penumbra of our lives,
the insomnia of children
who have gazed down the bottomless plunge of space
for the first time, lost
between the distant houses of the stars—

We who no longer even look up
at the night, we know him
nonetheless:
he is the broker of our confessions,
priest of our daily transaction
with the soil, the final executioner
of our will.

We have offered him our children.
We have offered him our grandchildren,
our great-grandchildren
down to the seventh generation.
We have sold all the children in return
for a wage to live on.

We have to put food on the table!

The man in the dark suit doesn't even know
he is the hunger
that lives in our bellies
and feeds on fear, he forgets
that inside his briefcase he carries
a huge, cold silence
that stifles everything but the light
of the television in so many
houses tonight—

He looks around from the platform,
momentarily mistaking
the President's applause for his own. Almost
lets a smile get away.

Premonition

Bright wings
fading in the gutter of my street

Spilled sunset—

*The first two leaves
to catch fall's fire—*

*One last flame flickering amid
a city of cold ash—*

Dead butterfly
fluttering against the grey cement
as the cars blow by

"I am thinking about the enemy gods,
    the enemy gods, among their weapons now
    I wander.
Ay-ye-ye-ye-ya-hai!
Now Slayer of Enemy Gods, I go down alone
    among them..."

        Navaho war song

Waiting for the Archeologists

Let us all bow our heads
and pray
for the evacuees of Fukushima Prefecture,
still making their mortgage payments
on the first of every month
year after year, even though
they can never go home
except for that one farmer who went back
to watch his cattle starve,
contemplating bitterly
how suddenly it can all
cease to matter

As another million-gallon tank
slowly fills
with the hot isotopes
of human hubris

*May God take pity
on the pride of inventors
the arrogance of engineers
the avarice of investors
the blind belief of the profiteers
and the propagandists
and the priests of power*

And let us never forget to pray
each night
that tomorrow won't be the day
some malfunctioning microchip
launches the attack
that has no sane response
in all the doomed
languages of planet Earth,
that day when we all cross our fingers
and hope to die
quicker than the rest

As the radionuclides gently,
invisibly
begin to drift
down from heaven

*Before another news cycle
flashes by, our whole vast
mercenary civilization
could so easily be
just another broken
bauble in the dust
waiting for the archeologists
of some hypothetical time
to come*

Ceremony at the Gates

We take our ritual positions
on the traffic islands
at the four corners of the intersection
smiling our
ceremonial smiles

bearing signs and banners of peace
at the gates of the apocalypse

The turkey buzzard circles patiently
overhead
like the unsleeping angel
of thermonuclear holocaust

Between Good Friday and Easter Sunday
the martyred Prince of Peace
descended into hell

We only stand waiting
at its gates
for the Saturday change of shifts,
offering our messages of peace
and possibility

Jobs in the thermonuclear holocaust sector
pay well,
keep the coastal economy alive
amid the endless wetlands
as the paper mills shut down

Thumbs up or thumbs down,
peace salute or middle finger,
honking, cursing,
each passing driver plays a pivotal role
in the ceremony of hope

even the ones who betray no sign

The submarines berthed beyond these gates
in the calving sanctuary
of the North Atlantic right whale
descend into the depths
off Saint Mary's Sound

Each three-story submarine a launching pad
for global annihilation,
each D-5 missile carrying a payload of two hundred
Hiroshimas,
each multiple warhead independently targeting
up to twelve cities

Their shallow channel routinely dredged
in a solemn satanic rite
to allow the passage of Armageddon
out to sea

We stand here bearing witness
at its gates,
representing the whales
and their declining young
and all the other ancient and newborn innocents
of this holy Creation

catching the sweltering April sun
on our posterboards,
angling it
across a blue line painted on the pavement
that marks the boundary
between legal protest and criminal trespass
into a nightmare netherworld

where the poles of good and evil are reversed
and diabolical warlords
rehearse for doomsday and then
go home to their children

The turkey buzzard circles hopefully
overhead
calculating the odds of peace,
of death, of dinner

One year ago, exactly fifty years
after Martin Luther King's own prophetic
martyrdom, seven brave
or ridiculous
or dangerously deranged Catholics

carrying hammers made
of melted handguns
and baby bottles filled with their own blood

cut the wire and vandalized
the unholy sanctum
of Mutual Assured Destruction,
that hair-trigger high-alert
suicide pact
between dueling genocidal empires

We only stand here
outside the base
projecting neatly lettered prayers for sanity
into the surveillance cameras
of the private security force that guards
the heresy
of missile-worship

until an affable deputy sheriff arrives
to shoo us across the highway,
from public property
to public property
under threat of arrest

as if the holy sacrament
of wishful thinking at the gates
of the inferno
makes the U.S. Navy nervous

as if our slogans
of demented optimism or obstinate faith
might somehow interrupt
the high-tech video game
called "Thermonuclear Warplanning"

might distract them from their daily drills
for a scientifically precise
first strike
of hellfire and brimstone
against their only world

while the humans assigned to carry it out
come and go

Twice as many honks and waves
as curses or middle fingers,
tilting the odds toward hope
for one more day

even though most of them betray no sign

The turkey buzzard circles hungrily
overhead

Kings Bay Naval Base,
St. Marys, Georgia
April 2019

Blast Radius

Standing here on the curb
outside the submarine base
with my stack of leaflets and my sign,
I feel like a hitchhiker again,
calm and relaxed,
posing like a model in an ad
for casual friendliness
and peaceable intent, swiveling
at the hip as the wheels roll by
to keep my sign angled straight
toward the passing
possibility of a glance— *"The choice
today is between nonviolence
and nonexistence!"* — M.L.K.,
abridged— aiming my gaze
like a peace-seeking missile
at the spot behind each tinted
windshield where I calculate
the driver's eyes watch the red light
and wait for the green,
smiling just enough to imply
*I'm having more fun out here
than you are in there, absolutely
no place I'd rather be!*
— not even especially impatient
for someone to roll down
the glass barrier that divides us
to accept a leaflet and trade
pleasantries, *How're you
doing, all right, have a great
day now!* — never once letting on
how deep and forceful
the blast of joy is that erupts
from inside every time
it happens, *Eureka,
hallelujah, praise the Lord,
I got a ride!*

Pheasants Waking Under Glass

When birds burst
headlong through the glass, small
soft harbingers of hot winds
fluttering on the carpet,
will all the blinded witnesses
suffer an enlightenment of sorts?

*We have constructed bigger crematoriums
in honor of our successes, we had
hoped to make the final payments*
            in time

Will we interrupt
our suppers, flapping up in a panic
like pheasants waking under glass,
understanding all at once
that thousand-mile-an-hour winds
could burst to children's blocks
the parliaments, the penitentiaries,
the mausoleums and museums?

                      Suddenly
*the Earth is a vast museum without glass
for the rest of time to consider*

Or shall we simply
pluck the feathers from the rug,
sweep up the fragments of sky
and sit down to discuss it tonight
over some scorched bird
while the furnace clicks on in the basement
and out in the back yard the missiles
lie awake in their silos?

*Over the splinters and sprawled brick
of two continents, a fine dust
of unforgiveness has begun
to settle*

"We have sold our shadow,
it hangs on a wall in Hiroshima,
a transaction we knew nothing of,
from which, embarrassed, we rake in interest."

    Gunter Eich, "Geometrical Palace"

The Weight of a Memory

We'll be better off without it,
some say,
this burden of nervous electrons
that strides so confidently down
the illusion of sidewalk
and cement—

A moment
of imaginary agony, they say,
and we'll go floating free
looking down with pity on the ones
still struggling in their skins.
Who can persuade the caterpillar
it's safe to kick free
of the cocoon?

Then we'll fly off
through the radiant strata of sky—
such a luxury of stretching,
no more laboring for food and breath!
—the Earth below us turning
like a wounded tortoise
lumbering on in blind circles
around the sun—

But what if we
remember...
birch woods at twilight from the lake
under a crescent moon,
ocean from the bluff at dawn
and the spouts of whales,
the embarrassment of blood
in delicate capillaries
as humans dance the dance
of mating...

We shook that body
    like a match.
We have left the Earth
    an ashtray.
We have traveled on
    like pioneers.

Even memories are not quite
weightless. In our subtle skins
we'll descend through the wind-currents
of a lake on fire—

One by one along the shattered street
the litter of dead are waking.
One, kissed by the cold sheets
of the nightmare, stares trembling out
through the new light at the window.
The rest get up and dress
for another day's enchanted
sleep.

Interrogation

How does it feel to be on the wrong side
again?

How does it feel to be the last to realize
there is only one side?

Is that why you give the empty thumbscrew
one vicious last twist?

Is that why you march your final prisoner
resolutely to the torn-down wall?

And what will you do when the handcuffed wrist
falls into bones and rust?

What will you do when the rags of your oppressed
lift up empty and fly away?

Will you lock yourself in your most opulent cell
with your electric cattleprod and scream
for mercy?

Will you serve your children cyanide to save them?
Negotiate endlessly with ghosts?

How long can you live on alone in your fortress
under the mountain, looking out
through the dead security monitors?

How long can you outlast the final assault of death?
Or madness? Or love?

(5)

Questioning the Interrogators

"The dogmas of the quiet past, are inadequate to the stormy present. The occasion is piled high with difficulty, and we must rise with the occasion. As our case is new, so we must think anew, and act anew. We must disenthrall ourselves, and then we shall save our country."

Abraham Lincoln, annual address to Congress (1862)

> "Life is no 'brief candle' to me. It is a sort of splendid torch which I have got hold of for the moment and I want to make it burn as brightly as possible before handing it on to future generations."
>
> George Bernard Shaw, speaking at Brighton School of Art (1907)

"I object to violence because when it appears to do good, the good it does is only temporary— and the evil it does is permanent."

Mohandas Gandhi, writing in *Young India* (1925)

> "With total wars a new element creeps into the picture. From now on everyone is involved, without exception . . . As war spreads wider and wider so will peace sink deeper and deeper into the hearts of all. . . . If the new kind of warfare demands that everybody and everything under the sun be taken cognizance of, so will the new kind of peace . . . A new conception of individuality will be born, one in which the collective life is the dominant note. In short, for the first time since the dawn of history, people will serve each other, first out of an enlightened self-interest, and finally out of a greater conception of love."
>
> Henry Miller, *Sunday After the War* (1944)

"II don't know whether I'll be able to change certain things for the better, or not at all. Both outcomes are possible. There is only one thing I will not concede: that it might be meaningless to strive in a good cause."

Vaclav Havel, *Summer Meditations* (1991)

> "Human history is history not only of cruelty, but of compassion, sacrifice, courage, kindness. . . . If we remember those times and places— and there have been so many— where people have behaved magnificently, this gives us the energy to act . . . The future is an infinite succession of presents, and to live now as we think human beings should live, in defiance of all that is bad around us, is itself a marvelous victory."
>
> Howard Zinn, *A Power Governments Cannot Suppress* (2006)

The World Travelers at Home

> for my parents, Doug and Carol Wingeier
> on their 60th anniversary, June 14, 2012

The travelers come home
to their mountain valley
with suitcases full of stories, a camera
overflowing with faces, the lives and struggles
of a world unknown to most of us
smuggled through customs
in their eyes and ears and fingertips.

Mom heads straight out to her garden,
Dad tackles the runaway lawn,
and all the while the voices
and hospitalities of that hazy expanse
beyond the mountain's green shoulder
seep up through the soil
from the other side of the globe.

Their little village on the lake
welcomes them back, that familiar life
of kitchen chores and mail to answer.
Still, between the smiles of friends
and greetings of neighbors a throbbing silence
accompanies them everywhere: the pulse
of hearts in danger, hushed breathing of the dead.

They tell their travels in words that burn
through clothing and flesh to the bone,
describe the sunlit scenery
and tortured politics of places they have seen,
show snapshots of laughing children
and shy young soldiers, pass around
the bloodsoaked currency of cruel regimes.

We can only listen and stare as echoes of a distance
far beyond our comforts and complaints
whisper through our hair and shiver
down our spines.   The gifts they've brought us
lie unwrapped and glittering in our laps: a greeting
in a language we don't understand,
the smiles of relatives we might never meet.

Happy Birthday, Buddha!

Sitting in the back row—
so many shades of grey
and white hair,
voices chanting
more or less in unison
a prayer for peace...
for peace to take root
right here in this room
approximately
                  now
and cover the Earth, a.s.a.p.,
with figurative flowers
and metaphorical fruit,
like the real ones so artfully
arranged on the altar
before us this morning,
making this whole
earthly plane an altar
and each day
an offering

News for You

Good evening!
Tonight's news is brought to you
by the poets of the world
and this season's migratory songbirds.
Thanks for tuning in.

First, the bad news.

Those people in Washington are not on your side.
Those people grinning on TV
are only actors.
The executives on Wall Street are loyal only
to the Caesars in their souls.
The generals in the Pentagon own concrete mansions
deep under the Rockies.
That man at the podium is selling you
your own flesh, pound by pound, and the net deficit
        which is all you'll have left
to bequeath to your heirs
is gnawing away at your bank account like a worm
in the belly of a starving child.

But wait!
We've got good news, too:

Death and taxes, weather
and traffic, none of it can touch you
inside
        where you actually live.
To sing, just breathe out more than you
breathed in.

        Listen, all the birds
are speaking this new language you have learned!

Hitler Came for the Gypsies First

Nazi grandmothers baked Christmas cookies
and knitted baby blankets

Hitler holds the all-time record
for mass murder, the history books say.
But that's because to get into the history books
you have to murder white people
and because for nineteen centuries
no one was counting.

Nazi gradeschoolers loved birthday parties
and kittens with bows

Hitler's reputation is secure
in the history books, and all over the world
Hitler's progeny are busy
replicating his mutant DNA, denouncing
whoever we're supposed to hate today,
valiantly culling the population
of the powerless—

Nazi teenagers loved going out Friday night
in the latest clothes

Hitler came for the gypsies first.
But somewhere deep
in the forest tonight, the gypsies gather
to dance and drum around a bonfire
while out on the roads
the state patrol, the feds,
the county mounties talk all night
on the radio.

Panoramic

First, gentlemen,
if you please,
line up here on the sidewalk
and strip down
to the skin.
Fold your clothing neatly
or just drop it in a heap.
Now stand
shoulder to shoulder along the curb,
arranging yourselves
from the darkest complexion
to the lightest. This
might take a little time, of course.
Just mill around
comparing the backs of your hands
with minimal argument
and as much
laughter and confusion as it takes
to find your respective
places
in the spectrum of skins.

Excellent! Well done.
Now link elbows and smile
for the camera.
Let the photographer
step back, and back,
and farther back until the faces
and bodies blend,

until the wide-angle lens
captures nothing but one long
continuum of color,
ink-black to chalk-white,
each of you all but indistinguishable
from your neighbors.

Now, you two
at either end, the Kikuyu
and the Swede, step out
into the street,
lead your end of the line forward
in a long arc toward the other
until you meet.
Reach out
with those awkward dangling
extraneous arms
and complete the circle:
chalk-white and ink-black
joined at the elbow.
Shockingly distinct.
Starkly opposed.
Clashing.
Contradictory.
Dichotomous.
Antithetical.
Indivisible.

Back of the Bus

Sitting
here on the long seat across
the back of the bus
with three other guys more or less
my size,
I can look straight down
the long aisle and see
the back of everybody's head:
I am
a minority of one here, swinging
wide at the corners, bumping
over the curb, ten feet behind the gigantic
rear tires—

A young lady gets off
through the rear door, stepping down
into one of the lurches that pass
for stops
just as an older fellow steps up
at the far end to pay his fare,
and I sense the huge, turning equilibrium
of everything

Vigil in the Citadel

Under a red sky
restless with light from the city
the flag hangs quiet.
Under its red, black and green
Mandela Center is settling
for the night.

The talk is quiet
but every so often a wind lifts the flag
so the words stand out clear—
"Nelson Mandela Center"—
and just like that every so often
the talk rises and other words
catch the breeze.

"Seventeen days until my first final—"
Someone mentions Strindberg.
Someone always seems to be laughing.
Someone at any given moment seems to have
no trouble sleeping.
"So they open up new steel plants in South Africa—"

This is a political occupation:
DIVEST NOW!
the signs along the walls are chanting.
The wind plucks a newspaper
from the concrete
and spreads the word:
"137 arrested at the University of Iowa—"

This is a test of our true learning.
It is a test of this university
in the name of the universe.
Someone has tied a red band around the clock tower.
It is eleven-fifteen of the sixth night.

May 1985, Northwestern University

Troy Davis Park

Eighty tents in the park!
It's a village
right here on the scuffed grass
among the hungry pigeons
in the afternoon sun,
surrounded by the downtown shops
and skyscrapers.
I can't tell which of the glowing faces
among this multicolored crowd
are protesters and which
simply have no other place to live.
Today there is no difference.
It's a village
of occupation, protest signs
leaning on the trees, an information table
staffed by eager smiles, a kitchen
under a green tarp
feeding anyone who's hungry for free.

Our new mayor won the support
of the downtown shop-owners
by pledging to clear the homeless from this park.
Meanwhile, the unemployment rate
keeps rising, eerily shadowed
by the number of home foreclosures,
oddly in sync with the statistics
of homelessness.
Economists are mystified.
But the rest of us
are beginning to catch on.

The owners of these shops around the park
are struggling, too.
Who isn't? Ask the owners
of the downtown skyscrapers.
What's the solution?
It's a village
of awakened souls stepping forward
out of their private worlds
into public view,
milling around on the grass,
talking in little groups
between the tents, raising their brave
voices against the plate glass and steel
towering around them,
feeding anyone who's hungry for freedom.

I don't know how the two loaves
and fifteen yogurt cups I brought to share
are going to feed this multitude,
but the people
have occupied the people's park,
I'm breathing liberated air
amid the downtown traffic fumes,
and I have faith.

October 2011, Atlanta

Election Day on the Vernal Equinox

Welcome, Spring!
I recognize your timid track
in the grey slush of an election day's
dawn, too late to catch you
stealing out in the vernal light

> *I speak as one who knows the forms*
> *of politeness to animals,*
> *the proper terms of address*
> *to the flowers— I speak only*
> *as one accustomed to carrying weight,*
> *the buoyancy of muscle, instinct*
> *anticipating changes in the light—*

Today we choose:
a power seeping through the sidewalk
and the soles of our shoes
wakes the worms and bugs in us, birds
start out of sleep in our heads and sing,
the wet earth blossoms in our eyes:
today we choose.

> *At last the reach of daylight*
> *equals the stride of a night,*
> *the dead face stirs beneath its sheet—*
> *snow melts, seeds are softening*
> *and hibernating creatures shiver*
> *in their depleted fat—*
> *still half-asleep, wrapped tightly*
> *in our winter skins we negotiate*
> *the old ice in the new grey light—*

Awake at last, cat-sure of our footing,
rearing back like trees we greet the Equinox:
breathing our steam, stepping into the hour,
we gather early on Election Day
to welcome Spring.

My Language and My Skin

I am a poor man.
I have only one language.
The bilingual refugees
who work the fields and orchards,
the multilingual asylum-seekers
in detention, facing death
by deportation,
they are millionaires compared with me.

But luckily
my first and only language happens to be
the one that matches my skin.
The language that conquered the sunset
and ruled the waves
with cannonshot and musketball and bayonet.
The skin that proved its supremacy
with manacles and bullwhips,
smallpox and whisky.

At my mother's breast
I formed my bones
out of the grammar and vocabulary
that spells out the contracts
between the masters and the slaves
even today.
It authorizes me to bully and belittle
the bilingual waitress with false documents
who brings my breakfast,
the multilingual professor in exile
from some foreign university
who mops the floors behind me.

From generations of barbarian forebears
I inherited this skin as white
in certain hidden places
as the paper between the words
of every worthless treaty ever signed.
It's my passport to travel
the global dominions of the dollar,
where dark-skinned people
with unpronounceable names
must learn my language to survive.

I am a poor man,
but thanks to my language and my skin
I own a single share
in the multinational empire of the billionaires.
My dividends accrue
in daily doses of self-importance, standing-to-sue,
might-makes-right, holier-than-thou,
despite-my-defects, and I-was-here-first.
Not to mention that magical charm
innocent-until-proven-guilty
and the smug presumption that it means
everyone.

I am still a poor man,
but at least someone is more
impoverished than me.
My black and brown-skinned cousins
so many times removed—
the good-humored grocery bagger who secretly
hates me, the fawning panhandler
whom I secretly fear—
all stare back at me through a fence
barbed with privilege
and electrified with impunity.

As long as we speak the language
of divide-and-conquer
and see no deeper than the skin, each of us
will fiercely defend our share
of hardship and scarcity.

But listen!
All these foreign languages
and unintelligible dialects
that have landed on these inhospitable shores,
how they swirl together
in a multitonal music of joking and laughter,
improvised and unrehearsed,
a symphony of voices
hushed to listen, speaking
one at a time
their testimonies of exploitation and abuse,
their humble contributions
to the wealth
of the wealthiest nation on Earth.

I am a poor man.
I have only one language.
But luckily
my brothers and sisters of other tongues
and skin tones
are cautiously, warily beginning to teach me
the art of translating language
into living.
We all have skin
covering our inner sameness.
We all have voices to sing our deeper
uniqueness.
Surely our boundless confusion of diversity
only proves how rich we'll be,
every one of us,
if we ever learn to share
that treasure?

Obstruction of Injustice

Somebody's sworn
testimony inspraypaint
rides the endless boxcars
across the prairie,
someone's unrepentant
confession clambers up
into the spotlights
of yet another billboard,
some anonymous crowd
of online avatars
overrules every objection
of the counsel for the defense
of the unforgivable—
Yet here we are again,
zip-tied to the bench,
charged with disloyalty
to a regime of treason
in the court of blasphemy
and slander. Hold that
sign a little higher,
friend, raise your voice
in window-rattling
harmony with mine—
we'll keep marching
till we flood these streets
with an incoming tide
of outrage, a rising
river of hope, hearts
pulsing together to the beat
of the chant, strangers
related only by diversity,
committed to the crime
of obstructing the unjust—

Even If We Fall

The loudspeakers boom out
one more inspired
call for peace.
I turn my back on the platform
to admire the crowd,
and it's right there in their eyes:
Yes, men can live as brothers
to their sisters,
neighbors can learn to love
their neighbors! Yes,
skins of every hue can bloom
out of the grass
of this brick-walled park
designed to conceal us even
from ourselves!
Yes, the irrefutable earth
beneath the grass
will hold us up, even if we fall—
And no, those walls
can never contain the truth:
it rings against
the marble and glass around us,
where the business
of lawful murder tries
and fails
to hide its bloody fingerprints
and homicidal lies.

October 2025

Questioning the Interrogators

1.

It's too shocking to watch
without looking away somewhere,
anywhere...
Luckily, there's always
another channel.

Are those really
Americans,
firing gleefully into the running
knot of civilians
from the open helicopter door,
fifty-caliber shells
ripping open the flesh, splintering
families?

It's too heartrending to listen
without getting up
and doing something about it,
anything, right now...
So when the music comes back on
after the news, forget about it
fast.

Can you even call him
a man, standing over her as she cringes
or sobs
or simply bleeds into the dirt,
into silence,
into invisibility?

It's too painful even to think about.
That's what the pills are for.
But your mind
has a mind of its own,
your thoughts keep circling
back again—

*Can you call any place
"civilized"
where those who brutalize the weak
are therefore
somehow
thought to be strong?*

2.

Imagine having nothing more
to be proud of
than the naked pigment
of the skin you were born in,
no better way
to prove your moral superiority
than assault and battery
or homicide—
such a tragic poverty of heart,
some deep childhood
deficiency, such pathetic
desperation
for a smidgen of superficial
privilege over someone,
anyone at all—

*How many generations of wealthy heirs
have inherited and re-invested
the dirty capital of the slave trade
and the plantations,
all this real estate appropriated at gunpoint
from Indians?
How much of our almighty
free-market economy would remain
if we gave back every cent of stolen profit,
with 500 years
of compounded interest?*

3.

For sale:
a waiver of immunity
from the ordinance or statute of your choice.
Prices start in the low tens of thousands.
Or, for a hundred grand,
invest in our expertly customized legislation!
But wait: this election year only,
a mere million will purchase your own personal
public official—

Can you call any nation
a "democracy"
where simply knowing your rights is probable cause,
where innocent bystanders are
strapped down
in the lethal injection chamber
to protect the rights of the police,
where night after night the evening anchorman
grants a full pardon
to the powerful?

4.

The gutterpunks and gangstas,
street people and road dogs,
the foreclosed families sleeping in SUVs,
the undocumented mothers,
incarcerated fathers, indentured daughters,
the suicidal veterans,
beggars on the freeway ramps,
roaming prophets off their meds—

They all know who pays
for the spit-shine on that stretch limo
cruising past the mouth
of the alley at midnight.
They all know what it means when over half
of our Senators are millionaires.
They know which offshore haven
hides the assets
of the world's most lucrative criminal racket.
They know what's coming next
when the bankers systematically
loot their own vaults,
like a mechanic who drains your crankcase
in the middle of the night
to buy a thousand hectares of farmland
in Africa or South America
and hire some mercenary government
to guard it—

What is a "human being," anyway?
How exactly do opposable thumbs
and an enlarged neocortex
justify killing off the passenger pigeon,
bursting the eardrums of whales,
spewing PCBs into the rivers,
burnt carbon into the sky?
What kind of species wagers its own offspring
against the sober prophecies of science?
Who are these two-legged
machines of avarice and pleasure
who think they can own everything including
each other?

5.

Since the victim is a woman,
no one calls it "terrorism."
Since the victim was a young black male,
no one calls the cop a "terrorist."

But what else is any self-respecting terrorist
trying to do
but murder one or two, or fifty, or five hundred
to terrorize the rest?
And what cause could be more holy
than the venerable tradition
of keeping blacks and women in their place?

6.

If the victims are desperately poor
subsistence farmers somewhere,
anywhere
in the developing world,
no one calls the corporate officers
and their enforcers
"a terrorist organization."
No one even dares to whisper it.
The satellites are listening.
The drones are watching.
The webcam on your laptop
monitors your facial expression
at every click of the mouse.
Your cellphone silently
turns itself on
whenever you mention the word "Koran."
And the prisoners at Guantanamo
go on waiting for their trials
like so many severed heads on pikes
along the highway...

Sorry, America. Torture *is* terrorism.

Can you honestly call people
"adults"
who sit watching from leatherette
easychairs and silk divans, cheering on cue
while celebrity hypnotists
and shadowy ventriloquists
pitch the latest war like a sleazy commercial
with cynical special effects,
the latest technology
for taking out an urban population,
uniformed
assassins for hire?

      7.

Because the winners write the history books,
the killer walks.
Because the audience madly applauds,
bravo, a standing ovation,
we think the show is over.
But outside the theater, the killer crouches
in the parking lot
with a nine-inch blade
and a desperate craving for caviar and champagne.

No matter which side we root for
in the Sunday football game,
the stockholders gulp down their dividends,
the CEO devours his annual bonus
and the babies on food stamps
wait all night in the Emergency Room
while their sleepless mothers watch the TV
bolted to the ceiling
and pray...

*What is this life of ours but 3-D entertainment
wherever we go, a menu of choices
from colleges to careers, a comfortable home
filled with useless luxury?
What is the world for
if not my own personal fulfillment,
regardless of the debt crisis
consuming the Global South,
the archipelago of plastic
circling the Pacific,
the unsuspecting pre-schoolers who'll inherit
the rising ocean
and the radioactive landfills?*

8.

The world has been known
to change.
It's called "history." Slow,
haphazard, blind,
every now and again
as sudden as an earthquake
or a revolution.
Which means, if you stop
to think,
the world just might change again.
Today. Tonight. Tomorrow.
And no one
will be expecting it except the ones
who stand ready any moment
to change everything
in a breath.

*Will the Americans ever be as brave
and free
as the towelheaded A-rabs were that spring?
As the Guatemalan patriots,
the schoolchildren of South Africa,
the stubborn partisans
of Vietnam?
As the fierce native defenders
of Turtle Island herself, from sea
to shining sea,
or the grandchildren of slaves
who taught this nation the meaning
of its creed?*

Ignore the screaming self-promoters
and the soft-porn hype.
Don't fall for the marketing buzz.
The so-called "holidays" are a scam.
Have you forgotten? Every day
is holier than the one before.
Be the person you always wanted to be.
Make the history you want to see
on the news tonight.
And remember, the one
standing next to you in the crowd
is the community you seek.
Put away your phone and let your eyes
explain.

In the Cracks of Babylon

Grass grows
only in the cracks here

*We used to trust the government
and the scientists
All those detectives on TV*

To protect and serve us they don't mind
beating up a few
to educate the rest, these bored
cops on overtime

*We used to believe our doctors,
ministers, professors
Even the actors in commercials*

Tape is cheap,
a satellite talk show passes
for company tonight, instantaneous
celebrities from space

*We used to trust the daily news, at least
the sports and weather
Now we don't trust anyone at all*

Giant presses somewhere
printing money just like science fiction,
trainloads of fresh bills
whistling past the bankrupt fields

*Everyone knows, money
isn't worth what you pay for it
Santa Claus is dead
We're not in business for your health
It's only criminal if you get
caught*

They took away our
power to live our lives
They did it
long before we were born

                                          But
we write the writing on the wall,
we are blooming in the cracks
of Babylon—

We had to teach you to survive
when you didn't know
what dirt was for

      Pause

      Sixteen working people
      waiting at the drawbridge
      while the bus pumps its diesel
      poison to heaven
      and a gull-white sail glides
      through the gap in sixteen
      working days

      As if each of us was
      a feather
                    lifted
      in the sweep of the wide wing,
      carried up in the beat
      from payday to payday
      though only the driver is still
      on the clock—

      Ah, but every one
      is a wing
      bearing up the other

What Democracy Looks Like

*Man scattering seeds
as excited pigeons assemble
on the sidewalk...*

Heading out to the demonstration
much too early
on a winter morning
windy even for Chicago, I wonder:
is he demonstrating better stewardship of seed
than someone like me,
forever confusing freedom
with speech, like vapor
scattering instantly in the wind
as it leaves my lips?

*Peace is not the property
of the privileged, justice never just the mercy
of the violent! Silence
reverberates between the soundbites.
The moral arc of the universe bends, weeping,
over its sleeping children
who will never wake.*

The crowd in the bleachers sits
listening, each
leaning on the knees behind us, waiting
for the woman with the megaphone
to give the signal to rise
in one body and reclaim our tongue-tied
grief, our toothless rage,
our duct-taped truths and redacted
principles
from the howling sky—

*Resistance is a legacy handed down
from mothers and fathers to daughters and sons
not always their own
ever since the first emperor clawed his way up
on the back of the first slave
and raised the whip—*

One climbs the flagpole
to depose the past, its stars and bars
fluttering helplessly against
our gale of voices.
Others topple the statues
of pious cruelty and blind injustice.
Still others start to build, block by block,
the new republic of the future,
the moneyless economy, the policeless state,
the new order of the sanctity
of flowers
and the safety of children.

I who walk free while others sit
locked in cages,
I who head back to my warm room
while others roam the icy streets, locked out,
my so-called insurance won't cover
a diagnosis of indifference
or despair. But nothing is incurable
as long as spring blooms again and babies wake up
already wailing...

*Let us render unto life
our living.
All we owe to death
is dying.*

The Echo of Loneliness

What is the sound of one hand
washing itself?
                         Just try it
next time you duck into a restroom
on the run: on your way out,
try to skim a second off your time
by washing only one. And the next time
you try to push the world off its
psychopathic course
                             all by yourself,
just remember that lonely sound
echoing off the tile.

The Whole Thing at a Glance

Turned the corner and saw
the whole thing
at a glance, carnival
on my right,
stadium on my left,
gold dome of the capitol
dead ahead—

Turned around and saw
dandelions
in the vacant lot
where an old brick building
used to stand,
in the pit of its cellar
a fallen tree
covered with new green
leaves...

Mosquito

Things with wings
will fly.
Things with legs
leap. Any direction is
"forward"
once you've chosen one.

Inside my heart right now
this room is beating:
the house is breathing through my lungs.
A city burns around me,
raging in my cells, a nation rises up
to cast off its shackles every time
I stagger from my bed
to my desk
and put my shoulder to the world—

Curled inside
the egg of a mosquito,
another universe waits trembling
to explode
into matter and gravity and light.
For a minute, humming busily,
I and the universe
and the mosquito are all
one insect.

The Palaces of the Poor

We shall someday
bathe in the downpour
and all our sins will
filter into the ground
from which we have raised
our living and satisfied
all this lust for metal

Across the desert
of our fields and silos we shall see
the arriving host of the poor
singing songs of an age-old migration,
walking upon the waves of heat
past the grain elevators, mounting
up from the parched earth
into their palaces of vapor
and light

We shall all dance
come the last day of this drought,
we will roll in the puddles
and stand again
baptized, laughing,
all of us stained the same
color at last

AFTERWORD
"Duties of the Witness"

> *"Is it not the duty*
> *of those with imagination*
> *to try to imagine how this must feel?"*

(1) Imagination in Action

Poetry is an act of the imagination: not just imagination itself, but the *act* thereof. Poetry is imagination in action. But can poetry be activism?

"Political poetry" is frequently dismissed as the practice of dragging poetry down to the level of politics— corrupt politicians, feuding parties, rigged elections— the poet as propagandist. But it also has the potential to raise politics up to the level of poetry: an act of imagination which reveals the hidden interconnections that link us all.

Imagination has more than one face, of course. The primary form it takes in the United States, from Hollywood to the *New York Times* bestseller list, is fantasy. The romantic fantasy of boy-meets-girl, the mythic fantasy of good-guy-vs.-bad-guy, the escapist fantasy of soap operas and sitcoms and the Broadway musical.

Our national identity is founded on the adolescent fantasy of "Manifest Destiny": the heroic wresting of a wild continent from savages, the innate superiority of everything white, male, and "Made in the U.S.A." Donald Trump's call to "Make America Great Again" invokes this self-serving fantasy of the glorification of war and the triumph of the violent.

But imagination is also the root of compassion, the capacity to willingly project oneself into other people's lives and surroundings, vicariously experience their experiences and feel their feelings. Arousing this deeper faculty of imagination, I believe, is the true calling of the political poet.

Political issues like war, poverty, and racism are often reduced to numbers— statistics, demographics, polls and percentages, dollars and cents. They can also be too easily elevated to the abstract plane of principles and ethics. Political poetry can take these issues back to where they started: real people facing real situations that engulf them and those they love, raw emotion in real time, real-life tragedy and heroism.

At its best, political poetry slips across the lines of partisan ideologies and attitudes to confront us with the actual people involved in a particular issue, people on both sides of any conflict, people we may disagree with politically but can relate to emotionally. It can place us inside the skin of someone we have never met, creating an unexpected opening for a shift in our habitual biases and priorities. It allows us to peer surreptitiously into the lives of people halfway around the world who are suffering or grieving or starving or courageously resisting, and begin to care about their fate.

There's another superficial gap that imagination can help to bridge. That's the gap between our self-centered complacency and our responsibility to others. Poetry can help to illuminate the ways we benefit from the plight of those people halfway around the world— how just relaxing in our easy chairs, enjoying our privileges, helps to oppress those who manufacture and deliver our luxuries at slave wages. What connects us with the impoverished and exploited of this world is not just some lofty, condescending compassion. It's culpability. It's not just a moment of empathy, or even outrage. It's a call to action.

But the poetic imagination isn't limited to the world as it is. Political poets can conjure up a hypothetical future, a better world... or hell on Earth. Poetry can be visionary, and poetry can be prophetic: two more faces of imagination.

The geopolitical strategists of the Pentagon have invested billions of our tax dollars in the sophisticated technology of nuclear holocaust. The executives of the industry euphemistically known as "defense" see only the colossal profits they are raking in. Both seem to lack the imagination to viscerally grasp the horrors they have unleashed by keeping the nuclear time-bomb ticking. But somebody must imagine it, and must communicate this bleakest of prophecies in language vivid enough to spark resistance to the ultimate delusional fantasy— "victory" in a nuclear exchange. This is the grim purview of the prophetic imagination.

But it's difficult to stand firm against the swaggering omnicidal beast of war and violence, or to stand up to the inevitable tyranny it breeds, without an alternative vision. Someone must keep alive the dream of a just society, a fair economy, a peaceable world to come, even a global renunciation of "Mutual Assured Destruction," no matter how unreachable it seems. Looking back, we can see how the personal convictions of individuals— the Abolitionists, the Suffragettes, the Wobblies, the organizers of Gay Pride— slowly rippled out to become recognized social norms, and were eventually signed into law. These evolutionary strides, which once appeared laughably unrealistic, are gifts of the visionary imagination.

(2) People's Culture and "Pop Culture"

Poets play a vital role in any authentic living culture. Throughout the Global South poets are heroes, quoted and recited and revered by ordinary folks. Poetry in much of Latin America or Africa tends to be political by default, either on or just below the surface, because in such places life itself is political; there is no place to hide from political realities. But the same is increasingly true among poor and working-class people everywhere. Only the moneyed classes can afford an insulating layer they call "culture" to shield them from the world of hardship and brutality.

"Culture" is one of the perks of the American middle class as well, in the form of "popular culture": cartoons and commercials, Netflix and MTV, video games, sports, sex, celebrities, a fantasy playground. In the shadows behind the screen, it serves the mercenary function of diverting our attention as the magician's other hand slips into our pockets.

True culture, people's culture, expresses what everyday people see and feel wherever they may be— a housing project, a refugee camp, a prison, the streets— and the anguish and rage that often erupt as a result. This is why Marley and Dylan and Lennon are beloved around the world: they speak to and for all of us, not just the literary intelligentsia, and do not shy away from political truths. Song lyrics are the poetry of people's culture, even if most songwriters prefer to traffic in fantasy, vying to make their mark on pop culture rather than plumb the deeper fathoms of imagination where vision, compassion and prophecy live.

In his essay "Leaping Up Into Political Poetry," written during the Vietnam war, the late Robert Bly introduced the poetic metaphor of the leap of association: "Some poets try to write political poems impelled by hatred or fear. But these emotions are heavy, they affect the gravity of the body. What the poet needs to get up that far and bring something back are great leaps of the imagination."

The disreputable reputation of political poets is not entirely undeserved; the temptation to get preachy and polemical often gets in the way. Hatred and fear have indeed inspired a lot of one-dimensional poetry, as have anger, self-righteousness, and hardline political dogma. But that's not the whole story. The American literary landscape seems ruled by an unspoken taboo, favoring poetry that confines itself to the personal, the philosophical, the whimsical, the abstract, the esoteric– anything that does not challenge the political and economic status quo.

But poetry was once part of everyday life here in the U.S.A., too. Walt Whitman's freewheeling free verse scandalized a highly literate nation accustomed to regimented meter and rhyme. His subject matter was equally outrageous, ranging from politics to sexuality to the daily lives of working folk. In his Preface to the 1855 edition of *Leaves of Grass* he wrote, "Liberty takes the adherence of heroes wherever men and women exist ... but never takes any adherence or welcome from the rest more than from poets. They are the voice and exposition of liberty ... to them it is confided and they must sustain it ... The attitude of great poets is to cheer up slaves and horrify despots."

But in the 20th century, mainstream poetry grew increasingly academic, enamored of classical allusions, intellectual abstraction, and the self-obsessed "confessional" mode. Until the political upheavals of the 1960s, the poets celebrated by the literary establishment were largely unknown to working people, disconnected from ordinary lives and struggles, uninvolved in the great popular movements for reform.

Step into the world of the poetry slam or hiphop, the cutting edge of poetry today, and the rules of academia do not apply. Many of these poets are using the tools of everyday language to condense their experience of injustice and inequality into poetry that is unabashedly political. They join a long line of rebels and upstarts, the progeny of Whitman: Carl Sandburg, Muriel Rukeyser, Kenneth Rexroth, Thomas McGrath, Meridel le Sueur, Thomas Merton, Allen Ginsberg, Etheridge Knight, Denise Levertov, Amiri Baraka, Audre Lorde, Galway Kinnell, Yusef Komunyakaa, Carolyn Forché, Martin Espada, and others unknown to me, I'm sure.

When I leaf through a copy of *The New Yorker* looking for poetry, almost without exception I find poets at play, writing enigmatically about trivialities, showing off their technical brilliance while dancing adroitly around substance— entertaining themselves, it seems, at my expense. I find that ironic, considering the in-depth political reporting often found in those same pages.

Word games, syntax puzzles, and clever special effects might help to sell a poem to *The New Yorker*— the pinnacle of poetic prestige— but what is the poet is trying to say? What is the poem about, what does it *mean*? Not "mean" in the sense of a specific, paraphraseable meaning, but in the sense that "It really *meant* something to me." Like so many of the celebrity novelists and nameless content creators who crank out the daily fare of pop culture, these poets seem intent on distracting readers from unpleasant realities, rather than waking them up to their potential as grown-up human beings who share a world with the rest of us. And unfortunately, waking people up grows more urgent by the day.

(3) Opening the Political Chakra

Participation in the political realm is only one dimension of living a full life. Yet without it, a twenty-first century human life is incomplete, like a body operating on only six of the seven *chakras* recognized by traditional Asian medicine. We are social beings, and any human society requires some form of governance. If we don't participate, we yield the right of self-governance to those who would govern us.

Like everyone else, poets have private joys and concerns: a personal history, a love life, family life, spiritual life, a relationship with nature, a connection with place and an urge to travel. But we also have a place in society, an ethical responsibility to our communities, a role in the economy that feeds us. Each person naturally values some of these aspects of life over others. But a large segment of the U.S. population has opted out of the political sphere entirely, disavowing even the right to vote.

Given the corruption, rancor, cynicism and deceit on constant display in the news, that is understandable. But in my opinion it is precisely this abdication of responsibility that has led to the atrophy of our democratic order, and it can only get worse. As Thomas Mann wrote in a letter to Hermann Hesse, a fellow refugee from Nazism, in 1945: "I believe that nothing living can avoid the political today. The refusal is also politics; one thereby advances the politics of the evil cause."

Like the non-voters among us, poets who shun the political domain of life are turning their backs on an essential piece of their humanity, and on millions of their fellow humans who are denied the luxury of making that choice. As the Trump regime pushes ahead with its authoritarian agenda, I think we will all find the political realm rudely intruding into what we once considered our private lives.

"If we give up the dimension of the personal," Carolyn Forché writes in the Introduction to her anthology *Against Forgetting*, "we risk relinquishing one of the most powerful sites of resistance. The celebration of the personal, however, can indicate a myopia, an inability to see how larger structures of the economy and the state circumscribe, if not determine, the fragile realm of individuality."

In Duncan Wu's Introduction to *Poetry of Witness*, a follow-up volume he co-edited with Forché, he echoes her metaphor of myopia, a tunnel-vision "peculiar to recent times," and adds, "Prior to that, poets commonly discussed experiences shared by the larger community in which they lived." Much American poetry today seems a bit self-centered, if not actually self-*censored*. Or are the traumas of family life here so extreme that they eclipse even those of a violent and abusive society?

We owe much of our culture's literary myopia to the way American military might has shielded middle-class America from the horrors of tyranny and war, even as our taxes financed those selfsame horrors in places like El Salvador and Palestine. The exceptions to "American exceptionalism" can be found in poetry by people of color, immigrants, prisoners, activists, and others often excluded from the Bill of Rights, and until recently from the literary canon as well.

Some of the poems in this book date back to what might seem ancient history, such as the Reagan administration's covert wars in Central America and the anti-apartheid and Nuclear Freeze movements of that same era. You'll find references to the Civil Rights movement, which I barely remember, and the Vietnam War, which ended just as I reached draft age. Unfortunately, none of these issues has truly receded into the past, and in the Trump era they are rebounding with a vengeance.

Under George W. Bush, we found new Vietnams in the Middle East to bomb, invade, and occupy. Under Barack Obama, a C.I.A.-orchestrated coup toppled a democratically elected government in Honduras. Under Joe Biden, my taxes continued to arm and finance a heartless apartheid regime in Israel and a merciless campaign of retribution far surpassing the Old Testament dictum of "an eye for an eye." As I write, Donald Trump's belligerent threats against nation after nation to divert attention from his authoritarian ambitions could escalate into war at any momen. And the threat of nuclear holocaust, though it has faded into the background of our daily political melodrama, hasn't loomed so dangerously high since the Cold War.

Meanwhile, the true greatness of America is under assault: the idealistic impulse that defied privilege and power to emancipate the slaves, extend the vote to women, grant workers the right to a decent life, provide for the sick, the elderly, the poor. A meaner, greedier America now proclaims that what makes this nation great is not democracy but empire—the ruthless invasion and plunder of a continent, the dehumanization of dark skin and the technology of superior force.

All of this is breaking news—but it's nothing new. The poetic imagination bears witness to what is happening down here on the ground, but it also soars high above, tracking the repeating patterns of history.

Virtually all of the poems gathered here were written before the ascendancy of Donald Trump and his cabal of billionaires. But their hostile takeover of American democracy merely ratchets the genocidal heritage of American empire up to a starkly visible new level. Trump is the reincarnation of every reactionary bully that ever stood in the way of our nation's evolution toward "a more perfect union," a multicultural haven for "diversity, equity, and inclusion."

The future of our republic is indeed in peril. But evolution is a force of nature. It may be forced to seek a way around, but it does not go back.

(4) The Poet as Witness

Political poetry plays another essential role normally considered the antithesis of imagination: documentation. The narrative we have swallowed with our Cheerios since childhood was shaped by the patriotic whitewashing of textbooks and the hometown cheerleading of the media. Yet we are accustomed to the luxury of dissent, and in recent years alternative re-tellings of the conventional American backstory have gained a foothold— military bases re-named, statues pulled down, Black and Native American and Women's Studies taught in universities.

But now it's our turn to confront one of the unmistakable trademarks of authoritarian rule, as foreseen by the Prophet Orwell: the "official story," with its enforced forgetfulness of troublesome facts. The Trump regime is determined to expunge from living memory the terrorism of slavery and the Klan, the hard-won sovereignty of women over their own bodies, the rich panorama of sexual identity. With shocking suddenness the newsreel of history jerks into reverse, erasing a century of popular struggle, even the clear consensus of climate scientists and medical researchers.

Yet the facts bulldozed under by what the victors call "history" can't be lost if the testimony of witnesses can be preserved— memorized, if necessary, when books are burned and the internet is censored and the corporate media obediently fall in line. The political poet bears witness to the victims of the victors, their lives and deaths and unexplained disappearances, and to those who march in their names to re-affirm the promises of democracy. Not in their millions, as a historian would, but face by face, voice by voice.

As a young poet, Carolyn Forché traveled to El Salvador in the late 1970s to work as a human rights advocate. After she returned she published *The Country Between Us* (1981), a book of poetry deeply scarred by her immersion in that country's bitter civil war, and an essay in which she declared, "It is my feeling that the twentieth-century human condition demands a poetry of witness." Her poetic testimony re-ignited in the Reagan era a controversy that had been simmering since the 1960s over the role of politics in poetry, and vice versa.

"Something happened along the way to the introspective poet I had been," Forché recalls in her Introduction to *Against Forgetting*. "My new work seemed controversial to my American contemporaries, who argued against its 'subject matter,' or against the right of a North American to contemplate such issues in her work, or against any mixing of what they saw as the mutually exclusive realms of the personal and the political."

The phrase "poetry of witness" soon took on a life of its own—"regarded skeptically by some," Forché later wrote, "as a euphemism for 'political poetry,' or as political poetry by other means." But as defined by Forché, it means poetry that inseparably fuses the personal and the political in the crucible of the poet's own experience of what she calls "extremity": war, imprisonment, torture, exile, imminent execution.

Against Forgetting (1993) collects over 700 pages of work by 20th-century poets that carries this weight of "extremity," most of it translated from other languages. *Poetry of Witness* (2014) adds another 600 pages of poetry written in English under similar conditions, reaching back five centuries. Both books offer only a fraction of the material their editors unearthed. This vast body of poetic work demonstrates that "poetry of witness" is a universal response to political adversity. It's not just "political poetry," Forché contends, or even just poetry, but *evidence*, documenting what we humans are capable of doing to one another, and what we are capable of surviving ... if we survive.

The term "witness" thus likens the poet of extremity to the witness in a court of law. But to me, it also evokes the Christian evangelical practice of "witnessing" to the unsaved. Though neither Forché nor her co-editor mentions this connotation, Duncan Wu hints at it when he quotes Forché's assertion that "poetic language attempts a coming-to-terms with evil and its embodiments, and there are appeals for a shared sense of humanity and collective resistance."

Poetry of witness expresses a fundamental faith that connection through language ultimately matters, even when the poem is discovered in a pocket of the poet's corpse. This, Wu believes, "has always been the means by which the imagination has articulated its response to war, imprisonment, oppression, and enslavement." Poetry, with its capacity to express "the sublime, the ineffable, that of which we cannot speak," offers the language "best suited to the task."

A North American visitor who brings back news of a conflict in a country not her own can be self-righteously accused of vicarious voyeurism. But no one can charge Dennis Brutus of South Africa or Claribel Alegria of El Salvador or Refaat Alareer of Palestine with egocentric exhibitionism when they forge their personal suffering and grief into poetic art. What, exactly, is the difference?

Forché has never labeled her own work "poetry of witness," as far as I know, but I certainly would. Her El Salvador poems document the suffering and grief of people whose stories she heard first-hand: flesh-and-blood human beings who live, love, and die there on the page before our eyes. The atmosphere of violence and trauma that surrounded her as she listened is palpable in every word. Just by taking in their stories, offering them sanctuary in her memory, she accepted a share of the risk they live with every day.

Lest we forget, the war she brought home to us was never just a Salvadoran war; we ourselves were funding the right-wing dictatorship whose atrocities she documents. Forché's poems pierce the reader's soul more deeply than any denunciation of "low-intensity warfare" in the left-wing journals of the day. Her essay in *Poetry of Witness*, "Reading the Living Archive: The Witness of Literary Art," concludes with this: "When we read the poem as witness, we are marked by it and become ourselves witnesses to what it has made present before us. Language incises the page, wounding it with testimonial presence, and the reader is marked by encounter with that presence. Witness begets witness. The text we read becomes a living archive."

In this context, imagination and documentation are not so antithetical after all. Poetic evidence that human beings have suffered and grieved can convey the reality of our time more truthfully than a news report or a political science thesis. Against the current of right-wing historical revisionism, the political poem becomes one of the indispensable ways our own lives, loves, and deaths can be preserved for those piecing together an honest picture of the past. The missing and murdered might return to us only through our imaginations, kindling compassionate understanding, prophetic horror, and visionary hope.

(5) A Bridge of Image and Metaphor

For me, poetry is a way of responding to what moves me and of grappling with what really matters to me, which are usually one and the same. Though I personally have escaped injury and indignity at the hands of the powerful, very little moves me as deeply and matters as much as the suffering of innocent people around the world.

Yet I have never consciously set out to write a "political poem."

Like any other poet, I write about any and every aspect of life. I have published a book of hitchhiking poems, and another chronicling my experiences at the annual Rainbow Gatherings. My most recent explores my deepening relationship with the natural world over the same four decades represented here. As the looming *tsunami* of climate change began to overshadow other concerns, this became my primary focus as a poet. Still, the cycles of crisis in the human world periodically blast my political chakra wide open once more, and a "political poem" bursts out.

Retracing her journey to El Salvador in *Against Forgetting*, Forché emphasizes that the poems she wrote there traveled the same route as any other to arrive on the page: "Like many other poets, I felt that I had no real choice regarding the impulse of my poems, and had only to wait, in meditative expectancy." The poems in *The Country Between Us* were gifts of the creative imagination inspired by searing personal experience, not statements formulated to make a point.

My own method is less meditative than serendipitous. When something stirs me deeply, a line or a phrase will sometimes flare briefly across my brain. If I capture it on paper, it might become the seed of a new poem, or find a place in one already taking shape. Calling me "political" only accuses me of paying attention, not just to butterflies and sunsets but to gritty and painful realities as well.

My work varies widely in form and style, though I have never composed a song, competed in a slam, or attempted the emphatic rhythm and rhyme of hiphop. My teachers are the elder poets of my generation, especially Robert Bly and Galway Kinnell, who broke the cultural taboo in the 1960s to raise their voices against Jim Crow discrimination and the war on Vietnam.

But my development as a poet took a breathless leap forward when I discovered Spanish-speaking poets like César Vallejo, Juan Ramón Jiménez, Federico García Lorca, and Pablo Neruda. Even in translation, their work conveys the politically-charged atmospheres of their respective times and places in a language of hallucinatory brilliance, surreal metaphor, and wrenching emotion. As a child of North American privilege, I do not pretend to share their experience, but their leaps of imagination have spurred my own attempts to new heights. Their concentrated intensity reveals much about the human reality behind abstractions like "oppression" and "imperialism."

My sense of connection with the actual people at the receiving end of oppression and imperialism was jolted awake by two peace delegations I was invited to join. My visits to Nicaragua in 1989 and Colombia in 2003 were experiences too powerful to describe in any form but poetry. From each of these journeys I brought home notes which I pieced together into a chapbook-length poem, one of which was published in my first book. The second appears as the centerpiece of this one.

With a few such exceptions, the horrors and traumas portrayed in these pages are not even second-hand but third-hand, gleaned from the writings of others or from faraway scenes flickering across a screen. My testimony amounts to hearsay. But if I can reach deeply enough into my imagination to grasp the reality of other people's lives, loves and deaths, perhaps your own imagination will receive *fourth*-hand the imprint of their struggle to remain human against all odds. In each of these poems, even those with a darkly satirical twist, I have done my best to transcend the political and penetrate to the heart of what is human. It's up to you to judge the authenticity of the translation.

I have had the honor of performing my poems at political gatherings across the Southeast and beyond. These have included annual vigils at the now re-named "School of the Americas" at Fort Benning, protesting U.S. military intervention in Latin America, "One Billion Rising" in Atlanta, confronting violence against women around the world, and anti-nuclear rallies at the Kings Bay submarine base on the Georgia coast and the Oak Ridge weapons plant in Tennessee.

One of my most memorable readings took place in the downtown Atlanta park re-named "Troy Davis Park" during Occupy Atlanta, using "the human microphone"— the crowd around me shouting back each line in a kind of call-and-response so the people in the back could hear.

I have written poems prompted by abominations like the school shootings in Parkland, Florida, the taxpayer-funded bailout of the megabanks, the fall of the Twin Towers and the made-for-TV travesty of "Shock and Awe." I have also written poems inspired by acts of resistance such as The Ribbon, a powerfully creative response to the prospect of nuclear annihilation, and the student uprising at Northwestern University to protest the school's investments in South African apartheid.

Both of those inspirational events took place in 1985, over half my lifetime ago. But according to Bly's essay, events— whether inspiring or appalling— are the occasion, not the source of a poem. "The political activists in the literary world are wrong," he insists. "They try to force political poetry out of poets by pushing them more deeply into events, making them feel guilt if they don't abandon privacy. But the truth is that the political poem comes out of the deepest privacy."

For its readers, political poetry may offer a public record, a trail of evidence. But for the poet, it taps the same wellsprings of inspiration and draws on the same reservoir of form and technique that all poems do. Compassion, vision, prophecy and witness do not spring from the times we live in, from revolutionary theories of capital and labor, analyses of neocolonialism or class war, but from what persists from generation to generation in the heart and conscience of the individual. Political poetry is simply the human in me, responding to the human in those caught up in today's headlines, reaching out to the human in you.

Can poetry have a measurable impact on political reality? I don't know—and if I did, it would have no measurable impact on what I write. We live in a time when more than ever before, all of us are called to do what we can to defend the defenseless Earth and its innocents. But Spanish poet Federico García Lorca, Chilean songwriter Victor Jara and his North American counterpart Joe Hill, Nigeria's Ken Saro-Wiwa and Palestine's Refaat Alareer might answer if they could. All died a martyr's death because someone in power feared the power of poetry.

But to question the usefulness of politically-aware poetry is itself an academic exercise. Just use your imagination. Imagine how different the world might be if poets had played the kind of role in the United States that they have in the humbler nations that have long been pawns of empire. If American poets had filled the literary journals with outraged compassion for the victims of lynchings and death squads, Sand Creek and Wounded Knee. If they had prophetically reminded Americans that what happens to nameless foreigners can also happen to us. If they had inspired their readers with the vision of a world founded on mutual respect, across all boundaries of race, class, gender and sexuality. If they had not been content just to write and publish, but had looked across those boundaries and built a bridge of image and metaphor in the words they chose.

As some in fact did, and still do. But not nearly enough.

Stephen Wing

> *"Is it not the duty*
> *of those with understanding*
> *to try to understand where this must lead?"**

---

*Quoted lines opening and closing this essay are from my poem "Duties of the Witness," published in *Four-Wheeler & Two-Legged* (1992)

"By recognizing our capacity to suffer with our world, we dawn to wider dimensions of being. In those dimensions there is pain still, but a lot more. There is wonder, even joy, as we come home to our mutual belonging— and there is a new kind of power. . . . As our pain for the world is rooted in our interconnectedness with all life, so surely is our power."

Joanna Macy, *Despair & Personal Power in the Nuclear Age* (1993)

"The power of spurious realities battering at us today— these deliberately manufactured fakes never penetrate to the heart of true human beings. I watch the children watching TV and at first I am afraid of what they are being taught, and then I realize, They can't be corrupted or destroyed. They watch, they listen, they understand, and, then, where and when it is necessary, they reject. There is something enormously powerful in a child's ability to withstand the fraudulent. A child has the clearest eye, the steadiest hand. The hucksters, the promoters, are appealing for the allegiance of these small people in vain. True, the cereal companies may be able to market huge quantities of junk breakfasts; the hamburger and hot dog chains may sell endless numbers of unreal fast-food items to the children, but the deep heart beats firmly, unreached and unreasoned with. A child of today can detect a lie quicker than the wisest adult of two decades ago. When I want to know what is true, I ask my children. They do not ask me; I turn to them."

Philip K. Dick, "How to Build a Universe That Doesn't Fall Apart Two Days Later" (1978)

> "America is still young herself, and she may become something magnificent and shining, or she may turn, as Rome did, into a black dinosaur, the enemy of every nation in the world who wants to live its own life. In my opinion, that decision has not yet been made."
>
> Robert Bly, "Leaping Up Into Political Poetry" (1968)

"The only cure for the ills of democracy is more democracy."
Edward Abbey, *The Journey Home* (1977)

About the Author

The son of Methodist missionaries, Stephen Wing grew up in Southeast Asia and returned to the States in 1970 to attend high school in the Chicago suburbs. During his senior year he boarded a bus downtown for one of the last demonstrations against the Vietnam War— his initiation into political activism. After graduating from Beloit College in 1978, he spent his twenties traveling the country by thumb, joining protests against the many outrages of the Reagan era along the way.

In 1987 he put his English Comp degree to work co-editing *Things Green*, a publication of the Chicago Greens. Two years later he met his wife, Dawn Aura, and settled in Atlanta. There he helped to produce *Street Heat* magazine, published by Up and Out of Poverty Now!, and the newsletter of a coalition of southeastern peace groups, *From Trident to Life*.

Throughout his years of activist journalism he also wrote poetry, much of it inevitably "political." His first book, published in 1992, included a chapbook-length poem inspired by a trip to Nicaragua, among other work on activist themes. The present volume collects nearly all of the poems he has written since that call for peace, social justice, and resistance to tyranny.

To pay his dues in Atlanta, Wing worked at a wholesale book distributor, then at a food co-op, coordinating the recycling at both companies. In 2006 he became a grateful cancer survivor. Now retired, he serves on the boards of the Lake Claire Community Land Trust and Nuclear Watch South.

Wing is the author of five previous books of poems and the creator of a line of bumper stickers, Gaia-Love Graffiti. (The title of this book is borrowed from one of his stickers.) He hosts his "Earth Poetry" workshop for poets once each season, exploring Atlanta's many protected urban wildspaces one by one. Current projects include an eco-comic novel called *Kumbu's Gift* and a monthly blog, "Wingtips."

To subscribe to Wing's email list, browse his published poetry and prose, sample performances and interviews, or contact him about his workshops, talks, and readings, please visit his website:

www.StephenWing.com

About the Typeface

Prospera, the primary font used throughout this book, was the first typeface to be designed entirely on a personal computer. It was created by my good friend Peter Fraterdeus in the late 1980s with the assistance of a grant from the National Endowment for the Arts. Its debut appearance in a printed book was my first poetry collection in 1992, and I have used it in all my publications since. Sadly, we lost Peter at age 66 to an inoperable brain tumor in the fall of 2019. His inspired calligraphy and other artwork live on at www.fraterdeus.com.

About the Illustrations

All my life I have been drawn to the art of collage. In high school I decorated one solid wall of my bedroom with a collage of collages on identical sheets of newsprint pinned up edge-to-edge.

From an early age I collected "found art" from streets and sidewalks, and later from highway shoulders as I hitchhiked around the country. I used it for a variety of collage projects, including the covers of a

series of poetry chapbooks I photocopied to give away in my travels. I have also used a collage technique in some of my poems, juxtaposing random fragments for aesthetic effect.

To illustrate this book, I scanned relevant images from my collection and assembled collages to introduce each thematic section. Facing each section's title page is an accompanying "collage" of quotations selected for the same purpose.

The collages on the front and back covers are likewise intended as commentary on the content of the book as a whole. The primary cover images are actual two-dimensional objects I picked up off the street—one in the United States, one during my trip to Nicaragua in 1989. You can probably guess which is which.

None of the scanned images used in this book represent an item I purchased for the express purpose of adding an image to my collection or an illustration to the book. All are serendipitous "found art."

—Wing

www.ingramcontent.com/pod-product-compliance
Lightning Source LLC
Chambersburg PA
CBHW051947290426
44110CB00015B/2143